D1283492

MAIN STREET MILITANTS

An
Anthology
from
*Grassroots
Editor*

Edited by

Howard Rusk Long

Southern Illinois
University Press
Carbondale and Edwardsville
Feffer & Simons, Inc.
London and Amsterdam

Printed in the United States of America

Designed by Gary Gore

Library of Congress Cataloging in Publication Data

Main entry under title:

Main Street militants.

   (New horizons in journalism)
   Includes bibliographical references and index.
   1. Journalism—United States. 2. Editorials.
I. Long, Howard Rusk   II. Grassroots
editor.
PN4726.M3   081   76-49522
ISBN 0-8093-0792-8

For all editors who published and perished

I am not aware that any law of my country forbids my sending what document I please to a friend or a citizen. I know, indeed, that mob law has decided otherwise, and that it has become fashionable in certain parts of the country to break open the Post Office, and take from it such documents as the mob should decide ought not to pass unburned. But I had never imagined that there was a sufficiency of respectability attached to the proceeding to recommend it for adoption to the good citizens of my own State. And grieviously and sadly shall I be disappointed to find otherwise. . . . The truth is, my fellow citizens, if you give ground, a single inch, there is no stopping place.—Elijah P. Lovejoy, in *St. Louis Observer,* November 5, 1835.

Contents

Preface   xiii

The Mighty Mice. H.R.L.   3

Great Lady of the Press. H.R.L.   7

Arrest at Church Suggests a Police State   8
    Hazel Brannon Smith

Arrest of Bombing Victim
    Is Grave Disservice   10
    Hazel Brannon Smith

Mississippians Break My Heart   12
    Hazel Brannon Smith

With All We Have   14
    Hazel Brannon Smith

Hazel's Pulitzer   14
    Hal C. De Cell

Alarm in the Night   15
    Penn Jones, Jr.

Weekly Editor's Obsession   19
    Robert Taylor

Recipe for Success, H.R.L.   27

Editor Fights for Good Government   29
    Gene Wirges

Report from Morrilton   32
    Gene Wirges

A Social Cancer. H.R.L.   35

From Knitting to News in
    Morrilton, Arkansas   37
    Kenneth Starck

More about the Mighty Mice. H.R.L.   43

Weekly Editor Campaigns against
    "Giveaway"   46
    Clifton O. Lawhorne

$4 Trillion in the Kitty   49
    Blair Macy

A Courageous Editor   51
    Houstoun Waring

Tennessee Weekly Editor Arouses Nest
    of Hornets   53
    Dean Ribuffoni

Monroe Placed under Moral Indictment
    by Shot Fired into Negro Home   58
    Dan Hicks, Jr.

Tell It Like It Is   60
    Baxter Melton

Bessie Stagg: Case Study in Advocacy
    Journalism. H.R.L.   69

Anyone for a Fight?   72
    Jack Fought

Gish   77
    Edmund B. Lambeth

Heroes, Living and Dead. H.R.L.   83

Confessions of a Failing Newspaper
    Editor   85
    Bruce Brugmann

Voice of the Little People   96
    George M. Killenberg, Jr.

Pedro Calomarde, Underground Editor   109
    Mason Rossiter Smith

The People of Clinton Were with Us   114
    Horace V. Wells, Jr.

How to Be a Man of Distinction 119
P. D. East

Sauk-Prairie Sequel 125
Leroy Gore

Crusades Are Not Cheaper by the Dozen 132
Mabel Norris Reese

Does a Printer Have the Right to Print
What He Chooses? 138
Lawrence Lorenz

The *Arkansas State Press:*
Squeezed to Death 144
Armistead S. Pride

A Company of Bold Riders 149
Edgar E. Eaton

Index 153

Preface

Editors of anthologies, I now realize, have no license to contaminate good things already written and published. Belatedly, I see my duty to destroy everything I have worked up for these pages, all the rough notes, awkward beginnings, gaudy hyperbole, self-depreciation, and quite a bit of material best described in the colloquial language of the Missouri Ozarks as "bank walking." Except for the formal credits, the thank-yous, the encomiums, and the how-come-I-did-it-that-ways, I find that fifteen years ago I said all that I need to say now in my editorial of the second issue of *Grassroots Editor* (vol. 1, no. 2 [April 1960], p. 2). Here it is again.

Even at this late date there persists the idyllic myth of the weekly editor as a poor man's Socrates who boycotts the church on Sunday, fishes through the week, and somehow or other, in defiance of the established rules of economics (and the credit association), manages to go to press frequently enough to retain his mailing privilege.

Still another stereotype reveals the weekly editor as one who has settled down at a lower pace to enjoy retirement from occupations of a more demanding nature, such as daily newspaper work, public relations, or government service.

Another view has him a job printer caught in the works of his own machinery and rendered incapable of coming to grips with ideas, once the end product of the printing press.

Or perhaps he is seen as a low-level politician purveying the pap of his party in exchange for county printing while begging for a tour of duty as local postmaster.

Or as a chore boy for the main street merchants.

Or as a salesman of advertising space.

Or as an anachronistic bankrupt.

Such stereotypes, in some instances, are ridiculous; in others, merely inadequate. A look at editors themselves, instead of editors as seen by people who are not personally acquainted with editors is something else indeed.

In the first place the man who edits the type of newspaper which may be called a community newspaper occupies a position unique in the realm of mass communications. It is a position which denies to him both the mystery enjoyed by the oracle of the metropolitan editorial page and the Madison Avenue craftsmanship lavished upon the public image of a radio or television personality. To his readers the editor of a community newspaper is the same man they see in church, at the high school basketball game, or drinking in the corner tavern. He is known for his good works and his misdeeds; for the company he keeps as well as for the way he treats his wife, his children, and his dog. He creates his own role in everyday association with the other people of the community. His strength and his weaknesses are assessed over and over again until there are few secrets in his personality. His place in the pecking order is known to all and in no way forgotten on the day his paper goes to press. There is nothing about printer's ink to obscure the personality of the man identified with this kind of newspaper. The reader sees in the printed page only the values already assigned to the man who produced it.

The weekly newspaper editor is first a member of the community and then a specialist. If he is a man who has won for himself a following, his is the sort of specialization which, because he has command of the printed page, enables him to project his influence many times beyond that of other men in the community who are limited in their contacts to those who can hear them in private conversation, in small groups, or even in public meetings. He has in his hands an instrument to challenge all of his capabilities.

Let us forget the weak and the inadequate, those marginal editors who make no impression in print or out, and turn our thoughts to the potentialities of that all too small group of weekly newspaper editors who are the kind of people who make themselves heard, whatever the company. Circulation is not too important. Small town, large town, suburban dormitory, they are spokesmen for people, and people are important. Houstoun Waring says three weekly editors who espouse a cause can win the people of their state. It may just as well be said that a dozen editors who know what they want, and who want something worthwhile, can set in motion a landslide of national, yes international proportions.

Now to tidy up the shop, *Grassroots Editor* came into being as a sideline of a sideline in the early days of the development of the School of Journalism at Southern Illinois University. I had arrived in Carbondale to head an unloved department, considered the weakest of the weak, just in time to catch the coattails of President Delyte W. Morris as he went into an orbit destined to transform a pretty good little teachers college into the greatest educational circus in America. Every administrator was a ringmaster whose part of the show was rated on his ability to generate viable brainstorms. Those who prospered were masters of the broken shoestring and virtuosos of the begging bowl. One of the early journalistic enterprises was a workshop put together with the help of Houstoun Waring of the *Littletown* (Colo.) *Independent*, already considered dean of American weekly editors, and Malcolm D. Coe, now of Bassett, Virginia, who had been my graduate student at the University of Missouri. We invited four or five hundred prospective participants nominated by schools of journalism heads and state press association managers as outstanding weekly newspaper editorial writers, ending up with fifteen participants from ten different states. The concept of a week-long retreat for editorial writers was not exactly an earth shaker, but for a handful of intellectuals and a few activists the opportunity to come to grips with the issues and problems of the day under the guidance of discussion leaders from the university was attractive. Each year some of the regulars returned bringing additional recruits, most of whom seemed adaptable to the system of structured and unstructured gabfests that continued almost around the clock during the week of these conferences. Out of these sessions developed such new projects as South-

ern Illinois University's Elijah Parish Lovejoy Award for Courage
in Journalism as well as the brainchild of the late C. A. Burley
of Menlo Park, California, The Golden Quill Award for Editorial
Writing. From the first session in 1965 there had been an informal
organization with a set of officers; Houstoun Waring was the first
president and he served two terms. In 1959 after Canadians began
to attend, it was decided to incorporate as a not-for-profit organization under the name, International Conference of Weekly Newspaper Editors. During one of the committee meetings, it was Houstoun Waring who remarked what a pity it was we lacked the funds
to start a journal. I responded by producing another broken shoestring in the form of the eight hundred dollars accumulated over
the years after the bills had been settled for each of the annual
meetings.

Where else but at Southern Illinois University could such lunacy
have been taken seriously? Professors Francis D. Modlin and
George C. Brown agreed to undertake to produce the magazine
as a class project for their printing students. An editor again, at
last, I collected articles from six states, Canada, and the Philippines
with a list of authors headlined by Henry Beatle Hough of Martha's
Vineyard. To these materials were added editorials selected from
the hundreds of weekly newspapers received in the Department
of Journalism, plus a page of book reviews. Thus when the first
issue of *Grassroots Editor* came out in January, 1960, the editorial
formula that prevailed so long as the periodical remained a quar-
terly already was established. Before the second number was issued
we had sold enough subscriptions to more than double our cash
in hand. By the end of the year we could afford the luxury of
purchasing our own set of Linotype matrices, Century Expanded
with italics and small caps. Because the printing plant was under
the jurisdiction of another division of the university we lost the
use first of the typesetting equipment, then of the printing press.
By owning our own type we could move from one arrangement
to another and still retain *Grassroots Editor*'s distinctive format.
We weathered the only real crisis in the twelve years of my editorship when a true friend, the late Howe V. Morgan of the *Sparta*
(Ill.) *News-Plaindealer* and one of the fifteen editors present at
the first conference in 1955, agreed to print *Grassroots Editor* at

a very low downtime price with the understanding that the work would be a fill-in when things were slack in his shop. This arrangement saved the life of our magazine but created problems not always pleasant to live with. In the first place a downtime routine was apt to bring out an issue four weeks late, two weeks early and hardly ever when we were expected at the post office. Moreover the platen press used for our work was capable of handling a signature of only two pages. It was just as impossible for one of us associated with the editorial side of *Grassroots Editor* to be present on Thursday and Friday of two or three consecutive weeks to see the work through the press as it was for the printers to drop their regular work for our convenience. These printers were fine workmen and devoted to "their magazine," but an editor without page proof flies blind, and his readers are pretty apt to assume he really is blind. It was a compromise to be lived with. When Howe Morgan passed on I was grateful his son, William H. Morgan, continued the printing arrangement that saved us literally thousands of dollars a year.

From time to time we sought financial support from various foundations, none of which was interested enough to act. Morris Ernst maintained a standing offer to buy a page of advertising with the bidding started at one hundred dollars and finally advanced to a thousand as a test of our corruptibility. (It had been determined that advertising at a reasonable rate would not be worth the bother.) The policy proclaimed by Delyte Morris as "letting a hustler go out on a limb and then propping him up just before the limb breaks," was the salvation. As Dean of Academic Affairs, John Grinnell would dip into his fund each year and transfer three thousand dollars for me to apply toward the printing bills. The practice was followed by his successors at that desk, including Robert MacVicar, who made a game of reducing the amount each year until I prevailed upon him to stabilize his subsidy at two thousand a year on the promise that I would never ask for a larger amount. Dean C. Horton Talley, for years would assign to the editor one of the graduate assistantships allocated to the College of Communications while at the same time including in the departmental student wages budget funds to employ undergraduate workers. Ralph McCoy and Ferris Randall, Library Administrators, contrived to purchase a dozen or two subscriptions each year to be exchanged with the libraries of other universities.

If former editors were required to read in concentrated doses the back files of their publications, suicide would become a more serious occupational hazard of journalism. The errors in judgment, the mechanical lapses, all the accumulated editorial sins are too much to take in concentrated dosages. On the bright side is the perspective developed as a by-product of the editorial task I am completing. The real bite of the early numbers seems limited to the sort of pieces collected for this volume. The "main street militants," as in retrospect I have learned to call them, became more and more important as editorial policy shaped up. Moreover this emphasis was an important factor in broadening and extending editorial horizons. Militant editors were knee-deep, even over their heads, in ideological issues. These concerns could not be divorced from journalism, no more than it is possible to say that different branches of journalism, as defined in terms of the media, are governed by differing sets of universals. And how could a magazine editor fail to respond to the stimulus of his clientele? Under this influence *Grassroots Editor* explored many areas not usually associated with weekly newspapers, as it became apparent that what concerns editors in Britain concerns editors in the United States, in the Philippines, and wherever else the English language is a medium of exchange.

Now I comprehend, as *Grassroots Editor* explored topics not usually associated with weekly newspapers, that what passed for editorial policy was merely my own fumbling efforts to grasp the same principles badgering the conscience of each of the outspoken weekly newspaper editors I had come to love and respect. It was no accident that *Grassroots Editor* became militant, too militant for some, not militant enough for others. If the test of legitimacy is acceptance by the Establishment, without ever intending it to happen, I was the editor of a bastard magazine. I do not pretend to defend all of the editorial policies for which I was responsible. Others have made this defense and some have offered apologies. Most important to me was the attitude of President Morris whose record of defending his faculty from outside pressures is unblemished. This is something to cherish as I wonder how many other state university presidents would have been so generous.

In the back files there is material for numerous anthologies, the press council movement, government and the press, the press in suburbia, journalism history, concentration of ownership, ethical problems of publishing, press freedom, and more. Strip away the ruble, and the mother lode becomes the ordeal of the editor of the small newspaper, who by his own decision risks all in order to report events and to express views that others would suppress. The cases reported in the magazine and repeated here by no means are inclusive; it is a shame that so many as deserving, perhaps, of recognition were overlooked. Nor is this collection offered as a personal glorification (much as they deserve it) of the people whose names are mentioned. There is about them a universality of spirit and purpose that repeats itself as a theme in a great musical score. Their combined stories in essence is the Everyman of journalism.

> And he that hath his account whole and sound,
> High in Heaven he shall be crowned;
> Unto the whole place God bring us all thither
> That we may live body and soul together.
> Thereto help the Trinity,
> Say ye, for saint charity.

All of the materials presented here appeared in *Grassroots Editor* either as original articles, editorial comment, or editorials reprinted from weekly newspapers. The decision to rely only upon text obtained from the files of the magazine is that of the editor. Resulting gaps and omission of facts valuable to the reader concerned with the details of record keeping is a calculated effort to balance fault and virtue. The value of updated biographical data on each principal (obsolete by the time the book is issued) is transcended by the importance of understanding the main street militants, not as the beautiful people they really are, so much, as prototypes demonstrating the problems of all people who would be free to read or write the truth untainted by willful adulteration. Specific bibliographical information appears with each piece.

When it comes to acknowledgments it is difficult to distinguish between those who contributed by helping to keep *Grassroots Editor*

in publication and those involved specifically in the preparation
of the anthology. This may not be too important because all of
them had something to do with the final product. But it is important
to mention that *Grassroots Editor,* although given in Carbondale
a home at Southern Illinois University, always has been the property
of the International Conference of Weekly Newspaper Editors, now
known as the International Society of Weekly Newspaper Editors,
and that the contents of every issue was copyrighted in the name
of the owner. Too much cannot be said about the appreciative
encouragement of the officers, directors and voting members during
my years of association with the enterprise. Formal acknowl-
edgment hereby is extended, along with expressions of esteem and
friendship to President Garrett W. Ray and the members of the
Board of Directors, of the International Society of Weekly Newspaper Editors for permission to reprint the contents of *Grassroots
Editor* from volume 1 through volume 12.

Indebtedness extends to all the contributors throughout my edi-
torship, not one of whom was ever paid for a manuscript, including
Professor Bryce W. Rucker, now of the University of South Caro-
lina, whose articles added so much to the crusading image of
Grassroots Editor. Most particularly am I grateful to Professors
W. Manion Rice and Mary Elizabeth (Betty) Frazer (now retired),
Mr. and Mrs. Adrian Combs, and That Lady from Arkansas,
Margaret (Carney) Long, all of whom have done so much more
for me than I deserved.

Other acknowledgments include Professor Richard W. Lee, University of Maryland, first graduate assistant to serve as managing
editor; Professor Clifton O. Lawhorne, chairman, Department of
Journalism, University of Arkansas, Little Rock, managing editor
as graduate assistant and later executive editor when he became
a member of the faculty. He was my successor as editor. Other
graduate assistants who served as managing editor were John C.
Taylor, who teaches journalism at Shawnee Junior College; Wendell
Crow, now a faculty member; Robert Smith, now in cable television
in Baltimore; Professor Harmon Morgan, Texas Technical College;
Professor Harrison Youngren, San Angelo State University. Judy
Roales, Washington newswoman, served as editorial assistant in
undergraduate days and later was executive editor under the name

of Judy Brooks during her faculty appointment. Professor Marlan Nelson, of Utah State University also was involved editorially when on the faculty here. I wish it were possible to mention all of the undergraduates who participated over the years in the drudgery of the mail room. Two of them, Robert Taylor, now in radio at Springfield, Illinois, and Guy Henry, Jr., whom I cannot locate were managing editors. Others whose names made the masthead were Richard Cox, *Readers' Digest;* John Epperheimer, *Ames* (Iowa) *Daily Telegraph,* Peter Workman and John Goodrich with whom I have lost contact.

Then I must mention the greatest of my teachers:

My sweet grandmother taught me to expect seven years of famine to be followed, Lord willing, by half a corn crop;

My bitchy grandmother ordered me never to cry in public;

My father, who had the willpower to hold his breath until he was blue in the face, demonstrated that the tormented can outlast the tormentors;

My mother showed me how to laugh when I wanted to cry;

And the greatest of them all, Walter Williams, convinced me that journalism is a holy calling.

Howard Rusk Long

February 2, 1976
Carbondale, Illinois

Main Street Militants

The Mighty Mice

■ Are they freaks or anachronistic throwbacks to the days of personal journalism? Where do they fit into a communications industry concerned about corporate images, debentures, and listings on the stock exchange?

They look like other people; much of the time they act like other people. Why can't they be satisfied to throw their weight around at chamber of commerce meetings and with making speeches to journalism students about Garrison, Lovejoy, and Zenger? Just why can't they be nice to their friends and ignore the crooks? Yes, the Mighty Mice of journalism are downright embarrassing to a profession with the kind of hindsight that can recognize a hero only at a distance of a hundred years.

Take that fellow Herbert Milton Baggerly, down in Tulia, Texas, who doesn't even belong to the country club set. But his editorials have made so many of the pundits look foolish that a respectable political scientist was inspired to undertake a book-length analysis of his work to learn why it is that the *Tulia Herald* rules the roost in the Panhandle.

Or sweet, gentle Henry Bettle Hough, whose craftsmanship is the envy of writing people around the world and whose serene language, on occasion, packs the kick of a mule. His *Vineyard Gazette* is an embarrassing reminder that good writing on newsprint is not quite extinct.

In contrast, there is J. R. Freeman, who writes like a blacksmith, but keeps digging away at what he sincerely believes to be one of the great scandals of our time. He lives in a trailer at Frederick, Colorado, and week after week is not sure he can finance another issue of his *Farmer and Miner*. Yet he continues to investigate what he believes to be a systematic theft of public lands bearing shale

Reprinted from *Grassroots Editor* 8, no. 1 (January–February 1967): 2, 34.

3

oil equal in value, so he says, to the national debt. And what will he get for his effort? A pile of debts if he is wrong. And if he is right, his only hope of vindication is that the big papers will steal his story.

Another little man, who also sang in the wilderness, with the help of a national magazine and the electronic media, finally brought his case to public attention. Long before the Warren Commission Report, W. Penn Jones, Jr., published in his *Midlothian Mirror* that something was rotten in the neighboring city of Dallas. "Pray to God I am wrong," he wrote one of his critics, "but we are far from seeing the last of the Kennedy story." Right or wrong, Penn Jones is giving all he has to the cause in which he believes.

Hazel Brannon Smith is a lady of the Old South who should be devoting her time to church bazaars instead of engaging in that dirtiest of all games, southern politics. To make matters worse, she seeks not patronage, but a respect for human rights. Her story of conflict with the White Citizens Council is an old one, her honors have been many, and substantial friends find a way to help her meet the publishing deficits. Nor is Hazel forgotten at home. Her latest incident involves a run-in with the state police because of alleged brutality in the handling of a prisoner. Was it a coincidence that the sire of her registered whiteface herd was found with a bullet in his head?

Yes, there are some gamy people among the Mighty Mice, such as that Arkansas jailbird, Gene Wirges who, instead of concentration on job work and the county printing, yielded to the appeal of some of his readers and undertook to clean out the courthouse gang of Conway County. This, of course, was a pretty bad mistake for a young man with a family obligation to get a ahead in the world. The politicians gave him the works. He was snowed under with lawsuits, which forced foreclosure of his *Morrilton Democrat* and finally resulted in his conviction on perjury charges, with a three-year sentence in the penitentiary, now under appeal. Gene's whole life and the lives of all his family were changed by this ordeal. But so was the course of history. A little man's revolt in Conway County may have been the pebble which started the Arkansas landslide for Winthrop Rockefeller and the return to that state of the two-party system. Gene continues to win his appeals in the state supreme court. And now Sheriff Marlin Hawkins must stand trial. Gene Wirges well may be one of the most successful failures of the decade.

A sweet lady, who knows judo, runs a tiny weekly newspaper in Mishawaka, Indiana. Certainly she is not in business to make money because she could earn more as a social worker. Somehow or other they named her the woman of the year, but the comfortable people are not really happy about Edith Boys Enos, because she makes them remember they are not uncomfortable. In fact, that seems to be the way she keeps the community working at problems most of the nice people would like to ignore. There was some rejoicing when a neighboring daily tried to run Edith and her *Enterprise* out of town with a competing sheet. But the neighbor went home and Edith is still in Mishawaka, pretending she doesn't know judo.

Out in Denver where a fight-to-the-death between two powerful dailies is now approaching the third generation in one of the nation's few remaining journalistic hippodromes, the best stories somehow seem to break in a weekly known as *Cervi's Rocky Mountain Journal*. Cervi is numbered among the Mighty Mice, although anyone in Denver who sports an outsize safety deposit box is inclined to speak of him as a rat. It was Cervi's reporting of cattle marketing practices that brought on the housewife boycott of the chain stores, and it was Cervi who gave the boycott its first real coverage. It was Cervi who reported the details of the struggle for control of the *Denver Post*. It was Cervi who challenged the manner in which Denver city officials went about renewing the electric franchise. In fact Cervi always seems to be around to interrupt when a man of affairs starts counting other people's money.

Dean of the American weekly newspaper editors is Houstoun Waring, who built a distinguished career on the outskirts of Denver with the *Littleton Independent*. Waring is the cerebral type, who without shrinking from direct action, has been able to project his influence far beyond the parochial audience. Like so many of his peers, Waring could have made his mark in any field of journalism. As his own man, however, he made contributions to society difficult to accomplish within the framework of institutional journalism.

These editors are examples of the species designated by Blair Macy, of the *Windsor* (Colo.) *Beacon* as the Mighty Mice, because as they scurry about the skirts of the Establishment, they seem to come to grips with matters in the public interest that escape the eyes of the giants of their profession.

When William Allen White chronicled the transition of newspapering into an "eight per cent business venture" he did not mention that the same amendment to our Constitution, which Gene Cervi says the publishing industry has seized as a license to print money, really was intended to protect the little man with a little printing press. It is the mice of the press, therefore, who are the legitimate heirs to the American journalistic tradition. Thank God, more and more of them are becoming Mighty Mice—H.R.L.

Great Lady of the Press

■ Down in Lexington, Mississippi, Hazel Brannon Smith edits a county-seat weekly, an occupation which has brought to her much grief, considerable financial loss, and many honors.

Mrs. Smith is typical of the friendly, churchgoing, home-serving women of the South, with one difference. She has a mind of her own and her mental processes will not permit her to accept popular stereotypes on the question of the relationship between the races.

Her troubles started in 1954 when the sheriff shot and wounded a Negro, a young man with no record of wrongdoing and who has not yet been called to face charges in court. Mrs. Smith printed the story, an account based upon information obtained, in part, from secondary sources, because the official in question had made himself unavailable. The next week she published on Page 1 an editorial of protest.

There followed a libel suit, and a judgment in the local court for ten thousand dollars. The findings were reversed by the supreme court of the state of Mississippi in a decision not for Hazel Brannon Smith alone, but for freedom of the press everywhere. This should be the end of her story as a crusading editor, but where passions are personalized, legal and moral victories do not always prevail. Local people, many of them honorable, patriotic citizens, were induced to enlist under the banner of an organization known as the White Citizens Council and dedicated to the extermination of all ideas contrary to the views advanced by its organizers. That which followed was warfare in which Mrs. Smith acquitted herself nobly, although, there are some who hold, too loudly.

After an election in which organized forces gained control of local offices, Mr. Smith, an able and cultivated gentleman with a master's degree who had permitted his wife to look after the

Reprinted from *Grassroots Editor* 1, no. 4 (October 1960): 2.

newspaper business, was removed summarily from his position as administrator of the local hospital. Mr. and Mrs. Smith were made the objects of a whole series of hate stories. Merchants were told to discontinue their advertising. Readers were encouraged to drop the paper. Job printing business was sent to shops in other localities. An opposition paper was established to take away the official notices of local government.

It was a bitter experience. Revenue dwindled. The Smiths were forced to throw their savings into the business; then to borrow money in order to keep the paper running. The fight is not over. Mrs. Smith's paper is still alive. Observers close to the scene say the tide has turned and that Mrs. Smith is now on the way to victory in the ultimate form of public acceptance.

Along with Mrs. Smith and her husband, Walter, the real heroes are the good people of Lexington, who had no personal identification with the issue, yet were unwilling to turn their backs upon the principles of decency and fair play.

Many of them, leaders and followers alike, refused to yield to pressure, else the cause would have been lost. To them it must be a great satisfaction to have in their midst such a woman as Hazel Brannon Smith—H.R.L.

Arrest at Church
Suggests a Police State

Hazel Brannon Smith

The state and national image of Jackson, Mississippi's beautiful capital city, as a peaceful, friendly, law-abiding southern community of considerable progress and charm, a city of good, God-fearing, and loving people, has been changed considerably, if not permanently, damaged because of the recent series of arrests of people attempting to attend church there.

The fact that these arrests have been of mixed racial groups

First published in the *Lexington* (Miss.) *Advertiser.* Reprinted from *Grassroots Editor* 5, no. 1 (January 1964): 40.

in a state which enforces legal racial segregation, does not alter the situation—or do us credit as a Christian people. The God we profess to believe in and worship is the God of all creation and through His Gift and the blood of Jesus Christ, we are brothers of all Christians everywhere.

Furthermore, freedom of worship and separation of church and state are constitutionally guaranteed all Americans. This includes Mississippi. Also involved is another freedom guaranteed all citizens by our Constitution—freedom from arbitrary arrest. Today these freedoms are in peril in Jackson and elsewhere in Mississippi.

A Jackson policeman has actually invaded a Jackson church and made arrests, charging four persons with "trespassing" and "disturbing public worship" (although at the time public worship was not in progress). One of the four arrested was a member of the church invaded. Two were Methodist ministers. One was a Negro student, a girl. Is this not the action of a police state? It would appear so. If not, it clearly approaches it. And it is with this we are concerned, the loss of our constitutionally guaranteed freedoms, more than the image we project.

Our contention is that every Mississippi church should be able to form its own worship and admission policies, free from coercion of any and all pressure groups, including local police authorities and the White Citizens Council, which recently issued a brazen statement of their own intentions relating to Jackson churches.

We should like to make it clear that we would not think of undertaking to judge a church for any policy it might adopt; no more than we would presume to judge or question the motive of anyone attempting to enter the House of God. These are questions to be resolved by Christians and the churches with their God, without help or interference from the local police or the Citizens Councils.

Many Christians today are troubled in heart and mind. Lifelong convictions and values held dear are being questioned in the current revolution which some secular authorities still refuse to recognize, much less approve. But we may be certain this revolution is going to continue, with or without our sanctions. The problem is how to resolve it.

If we the Christian people of Mississippi cannot throw off our fears and take the lead in solving our state's racial problems within the confines of fairness and goodwill, we may be sure that others less qualified will take over. And Mississippi will continue to be in deep trouble.

Arrest of Bombing Victim Is Grave Disservice

Hazel Brannon Smith

It is not moral or just that any man should live in fear or be compelled to sleep with a loaded gun by his bedside.

Holmes County Deputy Sheriff Andrew P. Smith's action in arresting a fifty-eight-year-old Negro farmer, Hartman Turnbow, for fire bombing his own home has come as a numbing shock to the people of Holmes County. It is a grave disservice to our county and all our people in these days of increasing racial tension and strife.

White and Negro citizens of Holmes County alike simply could not believe that something like this could happen in our county, that a man and his wife and sixteen-year-old daughter could be routed from sleep in the small hours of the morning and be forced to flee their home literally in terror, only to be shot at by intruders outside—then to have the head of the family jailed the same day, for doing the dastardly deed, by an officer sworn to uphold the law and protect all citizens.

The only evidence presented against the aged Negro man at the preliminary hearing was testimony given by Deputy Smith, and that was only an account of the bombing and shooting incident, as reported by Turnbow to him. Mr. Smith added his own opinions and suppositions, as did County Attorney Pat M. Barrett, who prosecuted the case. As a result the man was bound over under five-hundred-dollar bond for action by the Holmes County Grand Jury in October.

First published in the *Lexington* (Miss.) *Advertiser*. Reprinted from *Grassroots Editor* 4, no. 4 (October 1963): 9.

Mr. Barrett, who said he was "not a demolition expert" nevertheless told the court that "it just couldn't have happened. There is no way on God's earth for that situation over there to have happened like he said it happened."

Four other Negroes who had been arrested the same day in connection with the same case, were released for lack of evidence. Not one shred of evidence was presented against them. But they had been held in jail five days and five nights.

This kind of conduct on the part of our highest elected peace officer has done serious injury to relations between the races in Holmes County—where we must be able to live in peace and harmony, or not live at all.

It is distressing that no statement has come from Mr. Smith saying that he is continuing his investigation. Perhaps he is. We hope so. But irreparable damage has been done, and let no one doubt it.

We have always taken pride in being able to manage our affairs ourselves. When we become derelict in our duty and do not faithfully execute our obligations, we may rest assured it will be done for us. FBI agents and U.S. Justice officials have already made an exhaustive investigation of this bombing and shooting incident.

A suit has already been filed against Deputy Smith, Mr. Barrett, and the district attorney, stating these Negroes were arrested "on false and baseless charges," which were in effect an effort to coerce and intimidate Negro citizens of Holmes County and get them to cease voter registrations activity.

The federal suit asks for a permanent injunction to prohibit these officers from interfering with voter registration activities, including the prosecution of the charges now filed against Turnbow, who attempted to register to vote here April 9, and Robert Moses, director of SNCC, a voter registration project.

This kind of situation would never have come about in Holmes County if we had honestly discharged our duties and obligations as citizens in the past; if we had demanded that all citizens be accorded equal treatment and protection under the law. This we have not done.

But if we think the present situation is serious, as indeed it is, we should take a long, hard look at the future. It can, and probably will, get infinitely worse—unless we have the necessary character and guts to do something about it and change the things that need to be changed.

Mississippians Break My Heart

Hazel Brannon Smith

"It is not moral or just that any man should live in fear, or be compelled to sleep with a loaded gun by his bedside."

Those words are direct quotes from an editorial I wrote in May, 1963, when the home of Hartman Turnbow, a Holmes County Negro, was fire-bombed. I did not dream than that by October of 1964 I would be sleeping with a gun by my own bedside.

It was no news to me when the House Un-American Activities Committee in its current Washington hearings brought out the fact on Friday that certain Ku Klux Klansmen want me dead.

I was informed fifteen months ago by the FBI that I was on the KKK list and was told to exercise certain precautions. Some three months ago I received a special visitor from the FBI who came to warn me my life is in danger.

All my adult life—which has been spent in Mississippi—I have thought Mississippi is a wonderful place and that Mississippians are a special kind of people. For me there's no other place in the world—I want no other place.

So it breaks my heart to be faced with the indisputable fact that there are sadistic, morally depraved Mississippians who kill, torture, and maim other Mississippians; wicked Mississippians who bomb homes and churches; sick Mississippians who have added an unbearable burden of fear and terror to an already overburdened state.

The parade of witnesses from Mississippi before the House Un-American Activities Committee, most of them taking the cowardly way out, was in itself not surprising. Venomous snakes thrive in

First published in the *Lexington* (Miss.) *Advertiser*. Reprinted from *Grassroots Editor* 7, no. 2 (April 1966): 39.

dark, secret places, not out in the open where they may be recognized.

Well-documented evidence of inhuman brutality was read into the HUAC record, case after case. It is not possible that any Mississippian can longer pretend to be fooled by the Ku Klux Klan. Those who remain in it now must be regarded as the outlaws they are.

It is reassurring to know the FBI has the names of Klansmen in Mississippi and elsewhere—that the FBI has so thoroughly infiltrated the Klan it can no longer be certain its secrecy is maintained.

It is good to know Governor Paul Johnson has made a strong public stand against lawlessness and let it be known state employees belonging to the Klan will be fired. This is an example industrialists in the state might well emulate—it would put a definite clamp on Klan membership and activity if major employers in the state make it known they will not employ or continue to employ anyone who belongs to the KKK.

The state of Mississippi, I am certain, would not knowingly employ a Communist. Neither would any industry in the state. Ku Klux Klansmen have done more to incite fear and terror, hurt our state, and take our personal freedom away than all of the Communists in the world combined. They should be made to see the error of their ways, and straight talk from an employer concerned about the future of our state should have a profound effect.

Law enforcement officials, particularly sheriffs, should do more to identify Klansmen in their areas and put a watch on them. Few arrests in cases of violence stemming from Klan activity have been made by local law enforcement officials in the state. The general record is not one of which officials may be proud. In fact, local officials in some areas have openly sided with the Klan or winked at its activities. It is safe to say that as many if not more people are afraid of the law more than the Klan. I wonder how much worse things must get before they get better?

With All We Have

Hazel Brannon Smith

The thought of winning an award has never entered my mind on anything I ever wrote in my life—but it would be less than honest if I did not say that the Pulitzer Prize has made me very happy.

All we have done here is try to meet honestly the issues as they arose. We did not ask for nor run from this fight with the White Citizens Councils. But we have given it all we have, nearly ten years of our lives, loss of financial security, and a big mortgage. We would do the same thing over, if necessary.

As an individual, and editor, I cannot fit into the pattern of absolute conformity demanded by the Citizens Councils. I consider them un-Christian, undemocratic, and un-American. Their Nazi-like theories on white supremacy and their espousal of massive resistance to the 1954 Supreme Court decision have led the South and the nation to the brink of disaster in race relations and inspired the revival of the Ku Klux Klan. They have silenced many citizens and attempted to destroy those who do not agree with them.

I could not call myself an editor if I had gone along with the Citizens Councils—feeling about them the way I do. My interest has been to print the truth and protect and defend the freedom of all Mississippians. It will continue.

First published in the *Lexington* (Miss.) *Advertiser.* Reprinted from *Grassroots Editor* 5, no. 3 (July 1964): 6.

Hazel's Pulitzer

Hal C. De Cell

Hazel Brannon Smith of Lexington, Mississippi has become the third Mississippi editor to be awarded a Pulitzer Prize, which is

First published in the *Rolling Fork* (Miss.) *Deer Creek Pilot.* Reprinted from *Grassroots Editor* 5, no. 3 (July 1964): 7.

considered in most professional quarters as the ultimate recognition that can come to a journalist. We congratulate her warmly.

And while the subject of this Pulitzer award will be cussed and discussed, pro and con, across the state, we would hope that at least a small portion of fairness might somehow creep into the comments. And such fairness is to be found in the simple fact that the Pulitzer Prize was awarded to Hazel for her "steadfast adherence to her editorial duties in the face of great pressure and opposition."

This is undeniable. Whether you agree with her or disagree, it must be admitted that she has continued to voice and write her honest opinions in the face of cross burnings, boycotts, and all manner of intimidations which would have cowed a lesser person.

Regardless of her beliefs and how the majority of the Mississippi public may feel about them, it remains a fact that the fortitude and dedication with which Hazel has stuck to her editorial guns make her a standout among editors wherever they may be.

Alarm in the Night

Penn Jones, Jr.

A fire siren at night is always frightening to me. It recalls a multitude of sounds from North Africa, Naples, and many other long-forgotten places.

At 2:34 A.M., on the morning of May 1, 1962, the siren sounded more insistent, more determined to get quick help. "Keep those pants and shoes handy," went through my mind as I groped sleepily for my clothes.

I was racing to town when the fire engine stopped in the block occupied by the *Midlothian* (Tex.) *Mirror,* a weekly newspaper in a town inhabited by 1,521 souls just thirteen miles south of the Dallas city limits.

The night watchman yelled an excited "Yes" when I asked if the *Mirror* was on fire. Smoke was already billowing out of a large

Reprinted from *Grassroots Editor* 4, no. 4 (October 1963): 7–8, 35.

basketball-sized hole in the plate-glass front door as I fumbled for the key and opened the front door of my shop.

"Watchman must have broken the door," I thought as I rushed into the building and rushed right out again vomiting from the acrid smoke.

But why should a fire be blazing in the middle of the office area and on a concrete floor? There was little there to burn, nothing to start a fire there. But blazing it was, four feet high, and now spreading rapidly.

I ran around back of the building and crawled through the window, unlocked and raised the large overhead steel door. The fire was put out by the Midlothian Volunteer Fire Department just as flames were reaching the rafters of the building. A delay of two more minutes would have been a total loss to us of at least forty thousand dollars.

The fire was discovered by the night watchman at least twenty minutes ahead of schedule. Somebody had the watchman's route pretty well mapped out. Dallas and state investigators ruled it arson.

"Some mighty bad things have happened to Mr. Jones," an elderly spinster said as she walked from the fire that morning. "But," she added, "he has deserved every bit of it."

Yes, perhaps I have. The editor of a weekly newspaper who takes a part in community life and prints substantive news rather than just being a recorder has a pretty rough sled to ride. Ray E. Dover, editor of the *Valentine* (Neb.) *Newspaper* expressed it this way recently:

"Publishing a hometown newspaper has many complications, but being well-liked is not one of them. Everyone hates the editor. An editor who takes a firm stand on controversial issues, and tried to print all the news in an unbiased manner, may be respected (in a fair-minded community) but he will never be popular. Sooner or later such an editor will tread on the toes of everyone who reads the newspaper, be he friend or foe, neighbor or stranger."

In the case of Midlothian's school superintendent, it was sooner. Seventy-three-year-old Supt. L. A. Mills, who for thirty-one years has ruled our schools through confusion and evasion, began opposing my attendance at school board meetings as soon as he saw I was determined to find out what was going on. Mills made it clear that I was unwelcome. And meetings today are completely closed to the public.

The McCarthy era was also rough to take. Getting anonymous letters accusing me of being a Communist or a sympathizer, or chasing vague rumors to the same effect, is difficult to combat. Frankly, I'm proud of my military record of twenty-eight years' service with Texas's own Thirty-sixth Infantry Division, and the name-calling by unnamed enemies was difficult to bear.

The John Birch Society started its growth in Midlothian in 1961, led by some government employees, schoolteachers, and a retired air force major. I tried to delay any confrontation until after the important April school trustee elections. But delay was out after a Birch Society member spoke to a compulsory high school assembly.

When I asked that the speaker be answered, the high school principal not only refused my request, but said I did not even have the right to ask. At this point he started trembling, quit talking, and began punching. I was pretty soundly whipped that day in the office of the superintendent by the high school principal.

After further unsavory evidence on the Bircher turned up, I invited him to the shop to discuss the charges. Then my second fistfight in Midlothian developed—between the Bircher and myself. The fire bombing took place early the following Monday morning.

A couple of days after the fire, one city councilman asked the night watchman, "Why didn't you wait another fifteen minutes before turning in the alarm?" Surely we did not deserve that kind of treatment!

Papers, books, office supplies, and jumbled printed matter were knee-deep in the front of the 23-by-72 foot building. The entire place was four inches deep in water. Pictures on the office wall were water soaked and fire-damaged. A reprint from a *Saturday Evening Post* cover of Rockwell's *Golden Rule* was badly burned and blistered, but it will remain on our walls for a long time to come.

It was a blue and lonely Monday for the owners of the *Midlothian Mirror*, Mrs. Jones and myself. Since November 28, 1945, we have been running the newspaper in Midlothian. Our troubles began early in 1947 when I wrote an editorial critical of the city officials.

The fact that the story was true made no difference.

This is a nation which guarantees freedom of the press, and over the years we have spoken our mind and tried to tell the truth. But our words have been paid for in dollars and cents—for every unpopular word printed, we've paid the price in canceled ads and subscriptions. The fire was an indication that we almost paid twice. One of the compensations came recently in an editorial in the *Dallas Times Herald* which read:

"We've seen Penn Jones' editorials. They're stickery as a lawn full of grass burrs. And they can be twice as unpleasant. (He's not above taking a sharp chop at his big city editorial brethren, either.) But we glory in his being one of us—and we pray we can be worthy of vice versa. A newspaper must have enlightened belief in order for its influence to be worthwhile. But it must have courage in order to exist as anything worthy of the First Amendment. The need grows with the times."

To our then eighteen-year-old son, Penn III, the bombing was truly shocking. He stayed out of school and spent the day with us at the plant, sifting ashes and moving the sightseers out of the way. Our younger son Mike, then fourteen went to school, but it was a troubled and unpleasant day for him.

In fact, the day was a bleak one for all of us, but the next day we got a wire from a friend saying, "Don't let the bastards grind you down." That telegram helped, for we never did believe in quitting. "Controversial" is one of the nicer names given us by local people because I made it a policy to print the events at public meetings.

I have never made it a point to delve into private lives. I have made it a rule not to print first offenses and punishments of juveniles. I have told grateful parents, "All the kids get one free ride. I make no promises after that." One parent said, "If my son ever gets into trouble again, I will bring you the story."

As the editor in this little town, I have been insulted on the street, I have been run out of school board meetings. I have been threatened and evicted from city council meetings. I have been threatened many times, but the two fights referred to are the only ones during my seventeen years here—which is a pretty good record.

The most often asked question by curious sightseers after the fire was a bantering. "Gonna get a paper out this week?"

"By Golly, we will get a paper out this week, unless they can do a better job tonight," I answered, but I wasn't really so sure.

We hired our own nightwatchman for three weeks. He sat through the night with my pump shotgun loaded with buckshot. All was quiet—except the presses of America, which are now coming to our assistance. Papers across the nation have been great in telling the story of their tiny brothers, after that bleak Monday.

A two-thousand-dollar reward notice is still being printed here each week, and the presses of America have not stopped retelling the story of the bombing in Midlothian, Texas.

Weekly Editor's Obsession

Robert Taylor

His opponents are fear, money, and skepticism. His story is one some people are scared to read and many more are scared to tell. His reportorial technique is simple, yet complex—crude, yet sophisticated.

He has uncovered facts which lead him to say—in his newspaper, over national television, and in a book—that there was a conspiracy to kill President John F. Kennedy in November of 1963.

"He" is W. Penn Jones, editor and publisher of the *Midlothian* (Texas) *Mirror,* a small weekly newspaper of 725 circulation in a small town of 1,521 population.

He has raised question after question to national audiences about Kennedy's assassination and has been, admittedly, flying by the seat of his pants in looking for the answers.

His investigation at both its simplest and most complicated levels involves miles of travel at his own expense to knock on doors and ask questions. This pavement-pounding approach should not tempt one to believe that Jones's conclusions are similarly elementary.

The assertions Jones makes concerning the conspiracy, the inac-

Reprinted from *Grassroots Editor* 8, no. 4 (July-August 1967): 14-16, 31.

curacies and inadequacies of the Warren Commission Report, the strange deaths of twenty-one persons connected in various ways with the assassination and the prevailing attitudes in Dallas lead one to make suppositions as to the moral climate of a country which allows these events to go unquestioned. Jones is asking the questions. Therein lies his role in what he sees as the unfolding mystery of the assassination. The *Midlothian Mirror* published its only special edition on the Sunday following the assassination. Jones was working on the press getting out that "special" when he heard the radio "go wild" and he knew "something had happened."

He listened to details of the shooting of Lee Harvey Oswald and decided he "really couldn't believe it any further." As he now says, "That's when I really started to work."

Jones had been in Dallas on the day of the assassination. He had witnessed many of the day's incidents, and he began his investigation by organizing his own notes and recollections.

He then moved to question other newsmen from Dallas and the surrounding area about what they had seen, heard, and reported. All the time scanning newspapers and reading all accounts of the tragedy he could find, Jones was also urging Dallas newsmen to pool their efforts to report what he felt to be the truth. At best he met with casual assurances that it might be a good idea to do so, but there was little actual aid.

"I couldn't understand why no one else was working on the thing," he says. When Jones started his work on the assassination he found "more people in the state of Texas working on the Lincoln assassination than the Kennedy."

By reading almost everything written about those November days and watching closely details of the impending Jack Ruby trial, Jones says he began in early 1964 to get a glimpse of the story he was reporting and hints of whom to question and what to ask them.

He was at that time spending as many as four and five hours a day working on the investigation. This was before his work drew nationwide attention through the television and magazine media.

"Lately I've been working full-time. I don't work on my paper at all. I used to sell commercial printing, but I don't do that anymore. I don't do anything but go here and there to make speeches, or be on radio or TV shows, or sell a few books or read what other people have written."

Jones put in three weeks full time covering the Jack Ruby trial and questioning those participants whom he could. The Warren Commission Report was released in September, 1964. It took months to accomplish, but Jones is one of few who have read and studied the entire twenty-six volumes.

"When I started reading the report, I started seeing some things I did not believe," he says. "I think the twenty-six volumes and the report itself are an insult to the intelligence of the nation. The only reasons it's been accepted is because they sold a bill of goods to the press and the press of this country sold it to the American people. And they're still daring Jim Garrison to prove them wrong." Even though he is highly critical of the report, Jones still urges everyone to read it to discover its faults for himself.

The Warren Report and findings from his investigation serve as a basis for a series begun in mid 1965 which has run practically weekly in the *Mirror* since that time. Articles are either critiques of the report or interpretations of his findings in light of the report.

They have been compiled in Jones's book *Forgive My Grief* (vol. 1) which he printed on his own press. The second volume, coauthored by Shirley Martin, is due to be published soon. About the time the Warren Report was released, late in 1964, Jones first began to assemble the list of strange deaths he believes to be related to the conspiracy.

The list now numbers twenty-one and included among others Dorothy Kilgallen, who reportedly said before her death she planned to go to New Orleans and "break the case wide open"; Bill Hunter, a reporter covering the assassination who was shot to death by a policeman who claimed it was accidental; Tom Howard, an attorney who died ostensibly of a heart attack, without an autopsy, after Hunter had visited his apartment.

"I didn't think too much about the possibility of a list like this at first. But when I found that two or three of these people who died under strange conditions had known each other and been to the same places together—Hell, I knew it was more than coincidence," Jones says.

The people on this list presumably had knowledge of events

surrounding the assassination, and Jones will not let himself believe their deaths were coincidental. He further believes the list may grow.

This list, his theory of the conspiracy involving three rifles, his contention that the Warren Report is inadequate and that the FBI has withheld some information and failed to follow up important leads, his belief that Ruby and Oswald were hired patsys, his assertion that there is a highly wealthy group behind the conspiracy, his statements alleging involvement of the Dallas Police Department, and everything else he says or prints are the results of the answers he gets when he knocks on doors, the reading of press accounts and the Warren Report, and listening to others of his turn of mind. It hasn't been easy to get answers. Jones searched for two months for Earlene Roberts, Oswald's landlady. He heard a rumor that she was living on Route 2 at McKinney, Texas, and went to find her. A two-day hunt over the forty-six-mile mail route, checking names on mailboxes and knocking on doors where there weren't any names, failed to uncover even a trace of her whereabouts. She died before Jones or anyone could talk to her. Her death is one of his mysterious deaths.

"I felt certain Earlene Roberts would die after her testimony. I never did find her, but I know I searched for two solid months. I was not surprised when she died of an apparent heart attack," Jones says.

In the city of Dallas, with six hundred thousand people, there is one old man who helps Jones by studying police records and newspaper stories. He is scared, timid, and yet, says Jones, he loves his country.

An elderly woman came up to Jones during the memorial service at the assassination site in November of 1966 and volunteered information. Unfortunately her fears, added to the advice of her son, caused her to refuse to allow Jones to publish the information she had given.

"I certainly am an amateur at this business," he says. "And I was more so in the beginning, but I think we're making progress."

A gentleman contacted Jones following one of the editor's many appearances on television to discuss the assassination, with the story of what he had seen that November day. There are many such leads and many of them are unproductive.

Jones rode with Oswald's mother over most of East Texas one afternoon to no avail. He traveled to another city to talk with a woman who had called him. When he got there he found that she thought her house was "bugged." She proved to have only a vivid imagination.

Jones is still looking for a man named John Carter who supposedly lived at the rooming house with Oswald. He believes the FBI's questioning of the man was extremely superficial. There is no description of Carter or listing of his known associates or acquaintances.

Since a story on the private investigations on the Kennedy assassination in *Ramparts* magazine in October of 1966, Jones has been working full-time revising and further substantiating his theories— by knocking on doors and asking questions.

Jones says he meets fear at every corner, and that it is difficult to get answers from people who have been scared into silence. If one gives credence to Jones's explanation of the deaths on his list, the fear is real.

He has not been threatened directly. But he states numerous threats have been made to people working with him. Two newspapermen in Houston doing investigating work for him received telephone calls threatening violence and personal injury. Jones told them to pull off the case, and he lost his contacts in that city.

"I would hope somebody would be a little concerned if they tried to bump me off," he says. "But I think they're happy to call us kooks, Communists, and perverts."

If he were threatened, it is doubtful that it would deter him. He seems to delight in hearing that certain persons in Dallas hate him. "I'm complimented that they hate me. I despise the town," he says.

Jones faces another opponent in money. Those people he would like to question who are not silent because of fear are often uncooperative because, he says, they have been bought. Their silence brings a premium price.

Jones says people have been hired to deliberately mislead him. One man in Dallas supplied fact after fact—all false—in what Jones feels was an attempt to at least discourage him and at best trap him in a situation which would discredit him completely.

His third major opponent is skepticism. He points out that there is always a possibility that those people who have not been scared into silence or sold themselves into silence may not want to help Jones because they feel he is a Communist or a "kook" or even a lunatic.

Strangely enough this opponent has worked somewhat to Jones's advantage. It has led him into fraternization with the others working on similar projects who have also been labeled "kooks."

Jones feels that the work these people are doing is invaluable. He often recommends to audiences at speeches that they consider the writings of Mark Lane, Sylvia Marr, Shirley Martin, Ray Markas, Harold Wiseberg, and others.

The fine harmony of these investigators has led to discoveries Jones considers highly important: the "Miami" tape which reveals a conspiracy planned in that community to kill the president, his own discovery of proof that there was a Mauser rifle on the roof of the depository in which Oswald hid, and the writing of these people in general, most of which have considerable merit, according to Jones.

Penn Jones is still working on the story in a manner which is by his own description "without a plant, somewhat amateurish." He will keep working also by his own description, "as long as I live and as long as I'm making a little progress."

All the time he is asking his questions, the short but spunky editor makes speeches whenever asked, appears on national television, debates, and travels the country spreading the gospel of doubt concerning the Warren Commission Report and the assassination. If he can tell a few people what he believes and sell a few copies of his book to pay his expenses, he is satisfied.

"If I can find anyone I think I can trust, I tell him everything I can. I want this thing to be as widespread as possible," he says. "Hell, if it'll help this case I'll turn flips clear across Texas."

This spreading of the word Jones believes almost as important as the investigation. He feels that the American public has the right to know the story he and the others are telling, and that only with a questioning and informed public will the commission be reopened as he says, soon enough to prevent more killings.

Jones feels that "democracy cannot operate any other way—we've got to know the whole truth." This is perhaps the closest one can come to suggesting a reason for the dedication and devotion to truth which seems to be his standard and the flag on that standard.

Ironically, Penn Jones would love to be proved wrong. He would love to be the laughing stock of the nation ten years from now, because this would mean that the country he loves did not commit a sin of omission and commission which served as a prelude to its decay.

For all his questions aimed at uncovering details of his conspiracy and the assassination, there are two questions Penn Jones is constantly asking of the American public: Wouldn't you like to know? Don't you care? Nothing would please him more than to someday knock on the public's door and get the answers.

Recipe for Success

■ Take one young man. Stir in a bit of education, mix with ambition, and ripen with experience.

Wrap him up in a small town. Put him at last into his own business, well covered with mortgages and family responsibilities.

And what do you have? A conservative. Yes, and what else? A nonentity.

Older heads are free with advice: join all the lodges and the biggest church in town. Give a dime or a dollar to every solicitor. Work on committees. Be a booster, not a knocker. Stay out of local fights. Get along with people. Play ball with the powers that be. What's good for business is good for you.

Those are the rules for the young preacher looking for a larger church; for the young school administrator bucking for a bigger school; for the young lawyer hot after a fee; for the young businessman building up an equity.

The rules are the same for the young man who goes in debt for the privilege of editing a weekly newspaper. The older generation of his family says so. So does the banker, and the broker, and the man who owned the paper before him.

Tend to business, behave yourself, and everybody will support your paper. If he has any sense, this town likes to see a young man get ahead.

Gene Wirges knew the score: so much a month to meet the payroll; so much for materials and operating expenses; so much for taxes and interest; so much to retire the debt; so much, well a little at least, for family living expenses.

Get a good local girl to help you pick up the news. Spend your time hustling advertising and job printing; that's where the money is. And for Pete's sake, don't let some crank get you in dutch with the politicians.

Reprinted from *Grassroots Editor* 3, no. 4 (October 1962): 2.

A bright young editor, like Gene Wirges could have done a lot of good for Morrilton. He could have put his paper behind the Chamber of Commerce and the Ministerial Alliance, the Farm Bureau, the Boy Scouts, the Parent-Teacher Association and the Izaak Walton League. The town really needed a young hustler to help with the Community Chest, Clean-up Week, and the drive for new Christmas lights on Main Street.

There's no need to stir things up. Besides, you can't do a thing about it. Just keep your nose clean and someday they'll hang themselves. But you can't keep a good dog away from the birds nor a good reporter from coming up with the news. Gene got the news. What's more, he wrote it up. And all Hell broke loose.

The young editor's road to success suddenly became booby-trapped with lawsuits, foreclosures, tax sales, lost accounts. Wirges, himself, was beaten up. His family was threatened and his house was stoned. Wirges remains a businessman in Morrilton only because people from outside the county advanced money to satisfy the claims against his newspaper plant.

The county machine may be at bay, but it still is in power. To date, Wirges is a victor only in that some of the more honorable and least timid of his fellow citizens have joined his crusade.

Of course he battles on. Eventually the law will have its way with the wrongdoers and the people of Conway County will be free to rule, or to turn their local government over to another pack of rascals.

But look what Wirges had done with the recipe! What will success bring to him? Ask the efficiency experts. Ask the accountants. Then, ask yourself. Did Gene Wirges really let his cake fall?—H.R.L.

Editor Fights for Good Government

Gene Wirges

The first clash on the Conway County scene came in the June 6, 1961, city manager election. For months prior to that date, most of the town's leading citizens joined hands to effect a change to the city manager form of government.

There were many reasons why citizens sought a change from the mayor-council government. A sewer construction bond issue was defeated twice by the people then was passed by the council without a popular vote and finally didn't work. Besides, lack of management resulted in loss of nearly twenty thousand dollars in interest before the first shovel of dirt was turned on the project. City streets were potholed and otherwise there was dissatisfaction.

But Conway County Sheriff Marlin Hawkins, recognized leader of the county political machine, joined the fray and when the final vote was in, the city manager issue was beaten thirteen hundred to eight hundred.

Next was a special election, June 27, to decide the fate of Governor Faubus's proposed $60 million bond issue and to elect a new county representative. Loid Sadler, with machine blessing, opposed a local feed dealer, Houston Mallett.

Sadler won by a wide margin and Mallett was particularly disappointed in Catholic Point Township, where he had many friends and customers. The vote there was ninety-three to two for Sadler.

As editor and publisher of the weekly *Morrilton Democrat*, I visited the township and the first sixteen persons interviewed said they voted for Mallett. Fourteen of them signed affidavits to that effect. In addition, an investigation in Austin Township revealed there were more votes turned in than there were people to cast them.

Just before the *Democrat* published these and other irregularities, I learned what was meant when officials warned editors to avoid politics because "you can be embarrassed."

Reprinted from *Grassroots Editor* 3, no. 4 (October 1962): 3–4.

First, the prosecuting attorney called to tell me a criminal charge was being considered against me because of a "double mortgage" deal. "Go ahead if such a charge is in order," I told the prosecutor. No charge was filed.

Second, the chief deputy sheriff, Joe Guinn, came to post the *Democrat* for sale because of delinquent employment security taxes. This seemed strange since my wife and bookkeeper, Betty, had made an agreement with the Employment Security Division only three days before. The taxes were paid and there was no sale.

Another election was on tap—this time to select a new mayor and four aldermen in the Democratic primary July 25. Citizens backed a candidate for each post but the machine came through again in solid fashion. Two election contests followed and one went to the Arkansas Supreme Court. The supreme court reversed the lower court dismissal and ordered the case back for trial.

The political pot continued to simmer coming to a boil in the 1962 summer Democratic primary. There had been no contests for county office for ten years. Prospective candidates who were not backed by the machine simply didn't run.

An old-timer had told me, "Son, we don't have elections here. We have selections."

For the July Democratic primary, five county officers had opposition—including Sheriff Hawkins. Another big race on the ticket was for prosecuting attorney, a post held by machine-backed George F. Hartje, Jr.

Machine supports boldly bragged that opposition candidates would get "less than six hundred votes." But in the final analysis, Hartje was defeated soundly by a vigorous, young attorney, Jeff Mobley, who attacked Hawkins and machine rule as his campaign strategy. Other county candidates lost, but averaged nearly two thousand votes each. Such countywide opposition generally was regarded as a defeat for the machine.

Hartje, incidentally, had been prosecutor when the grand jury was called in Conway County in 1961. Other citizens joined me in taking about eighty charges of election law violations and irregularities to the grand jury. There was little doubt about the outcome, however, with half-a-dozen jurors having served as officials in the elections to be investigated. I was threatened with indictments for contempt and libel and, in the end, the jury returned no true bills.

The grand jury officially admitted, in its report, that the violations and irregularities existed but excused them because election officials were "ignorant of the law" or because the acts were "customary." It was, of course, a statewide laughingstock.

Efforts to halt the *Democrat*'s "crusade" for better government and honest elections haven't stopped. Not by any means.

Advertisers were contacted and pressured. The same happened to country correspondents, subscribers, and commercial printing customers. In addition, employees of the *Morrilton Democrat* repeatedly were advised to quit their jobs and or leave town. Some did.

The most recent addition to the staff is a twenty-three-year-old Les Seago, an air force veteran. Two days after coming to town he was leaving the courthouse when a bulky individual grabbed him by the leg and demanded to know if he was "Wirges's new man." Seago said he was and the man growled that "you don't know what you're getting into." Then he suggested Seago would be better off if he changed jobs.

Shortly before the July (1962) Democratic primary a circuit court judgment for $11,399 was entered against me and Sheriff Hawkins sought to enforce immediate collection—again my newspaper was posted for sale.

The sale was scheduled July 5 but was averted on July 4 (Independence Day) when Dr. Stanley Gutowski of neighboring Perry County stepped in and bought the judgment. He said he had done so because "I have been to Russia and we don't need boss rule here."

Even so, Hawkins refused to cancel the sale because his costs hadn't been paid. Then Hawkins refused to divulge the amount of costs due. Eight minutes before sale time, he did so through his attorney and they were paid under protest. As a result of all this, I have:

1. Sued 220-pound County Tax Assessor W.O. Hice for $31,500 for having assaulted me on Morrilton's main street.

2. Sued Sheriff Hawkins for $150,000 for "officious intermeddling" in my personal affairs.

3. Sued the opposition newspaper, *Headlight,* for $5,000 for invasion of privacy and libelous defamation for printing stories alleged to be untrue.

4. Sued Sheriff Hawkins for recovery of four-fifths of the $528 he had assessed in costs July 5.

I was once nearly mobbed at the Courthouse by a machine crowd, and my home was stoned later that night. A few weeks ago, the machine held a political rally and made inflammatory speeches about the editor. Later that night, a bottle came crashing through the plate-glass window in the front of the newspaper editorial office.

Now, elections are again on tap. In October, the people will vote on a proposed bond issue for industrial expansion. In November at the general election, the vote will be on a local option (wet-dry) issue; GOP gubernatorial and senatorial opposition to Democratic incumbents; and there are indications write-ins may appear to oppose the machine nominees. In December, two school board positions will be up for decision and there'll be a millage increase as well.

Presently, the principal attention is on November. And folks again may be asked to decide whether to retain the same officials who have been in control for more than a decade, or select new ones.

After the Democratic primary, a farmer came to the *Democrat* office and put it this way, "Don't give up now, Mr. Wirges, we have just begun to fight."

Report from Morrilton

Gene Wirges

You'll recall that last year, I told you our group—Better Government League—hadn't supported a winner in any of our elections, even though there had been eight or ten of them. And you'll recall another election was coming shortly after the conference. Well, we battled hard with these results:

Reprinted from *Grassroots Editor* 4, no. 4 (October 1963): 11.

1. The man we supported for the important prosecuting attorney position was a winner, even though he lost about 10-1 in our normal bulging absentee box.

2. About one-third of the township committeeman candidates we supported won on the basis of local balloting; but the heavy lopsided absentee votes put all machine-sponsored incumbents back into office except two.

3. Of the two committeeman winners, one left town about two months later, partly because of local pressure from politicians. The second, a lifelong Democrat, was declared by the local Democratic Central Committee to be a Republican and was denied certification. One lawsuit won him certification and then the committee denied him a seat. Another lawsuit brought a court opinion that he should be seated, but it hasn't actually happened as of this writing.

4. On the heels of the Lovejoy Award, I was honored by the Texas Southern University and received its Laymen's Citation for distinguished service in the public journals.

5. Our attacks continued on city and county shenanigans and the city clerk went berserk, trying to burn down my newspaper plant at two o'clock one morning. An attempt also was aimed at my car and myself. All three efforts were unsuccessful as police nabbed the clerk, wearing a stocking mask and disguise, in the try. She was shipped off before daybreak to a mental institution.

6. We filed, or helped to file, half a dozen more lawsuits aimed at breaking up various governmental inequities—all cases are still pending.

7. I was called before the irate circuit judge and was sworn in as a witness. Thereafter followed a forty-minute episode for which I have no description. There was no charge. The judge and I argued heatedly for the full length and a court reporter recorded the event. My efforts to secure a copy for publication have been unsuccessful for the last five months.

8. I have continued to investigate absentee voting practices and have uncovered a number of cases where people have been voting simultaneously here and in other states. All this data has been turned over to the U.S. Attorney's Office, the FBI Department of Justice and the local prosecuting attorney (yep, the one we helped to elect). The federal investigators still haven't reported their find-

ings and the local prosecutor currently is stalling. The latter development doesn't look good, to say the least.

9. Audit investigations of my own have turned up the fact that our county judge, in 1962, spent fifty thousand dollars more than was appropriated by county quorum court—an outright violation of state statutes. This was turned over to the prosecutor, and again, no action has been taken.

10. An investigation followed a school election in one of our districts last December, particularly in regard to absentee voting. Many affidavits were secured from persons who "saw no ballot at all" or "didn't request or sign any application" or who just hadn't voted in ten years or more. This data too has been turned over to the prosecutor. No action.

I faced an eleven thousand dollar judgment which was paid by a gracious neighbor in an adjoining county—Dr. Stanley Gutowski. The local sheriff, head of the machine, seized the check and the federal government stepped in and threatened to close my plant because of back taxes. At this point, another gracious neighbor—Winthrop Rockefeller, no less—stepped in to keep us running, guaranteeing the debt to the government. So you see, I've been a very lucky fellow at that.

A Social Cancer

■ It is not a pretty thing to sit through a judicial devil's mass and to watch a man railroaded to the penitentiary.

"Old Gene owes the state a thousand acres of cotton chopping," said one courtroom spectator.

"We'll get him this time," said another.

During a recess one of the veniremen, who later sat in the box as one of the "twelve good men and true," exulted to another, "now they've got only one challenge left."

Father Anthony F. Lachowsky, the local parish priest testified: "Human nature is one of those things we all have. We can't help having our opinions—there are varying sides of the opinion. It is very difficult to put aside our human nature on these things. Human nature being what it is I do not believe Gene Wirges can receive a fair trial in Conway County."

The prosecutor said: "Do you as a prospective juror in this case feel that you can examine the evidence fairly and impartially and render a verdict in favor of the defendant, unless the state proves his guilt without a reasonable doubt? And by the same token will you vote for his conviction if the evidence proves his guilt?"

The man who later agreed to convict Gene Wirges hesitated and then blurted out, "I would hate to go against my friend Sheriff Hawkins." Cross-examination revealed that he had a son of his own facing a murder charge in the same court.

When pressed by the judge if he could decide according to his conscience he shouted, "I will, I will, I will!"

Sheriff Marlin Hawkins, alleged kingfish of Conway County, was all over the courtroom conferring with the prosecutors, the judge, the witnesses, the veniremen, and members of his staff. At other times he controlled the action with hand signals, like the playmaker of a basketball team.

Finally, when the defense objected to the sheriff's behavior he

Reprinted from *Grassroots Editor* 7, no. 2 (April 1966): 2–3.

withdrew as official bailiff, but continued his movements to all parts of the courtroom, including the bench. A second protest removed Hawkins from the courtroom. But this did not keep the jurors from conferring with him in another part of the courthouse during the trial's frequent recesses.

Friends of Gene Wirges also were in the courtroom. Six of them, along with Gene, are under indictment for conspiring to bring charges against Sheriff Hawkins for alleged misappropriation of fines levied in traffic cases.

One of the Wirges partisans, a farmer with the appearance of being comfortably well off, remarked, "the only protection I have in this county are the loaded guns I keep in my house." Another friend of the defendant declared, "They don't have to make a case to get a conviction. Every man in that jury box has a connection."

And so the parody proceeded. Without anything that resembled proof beyond reasonable doubt, Gene Wirges, former editor of the *Morrilton* (Ark.) *Democrat,* was convicted of perjury and sentenced to three years in the penitentiary. Of course the case will be appealed.

Said the nice old lady who operates the restaurant: "Please don't be too hard on Morrilton. After all the South has had enough bad publicity. You just don't understand how things are in our county." But lady, we do understand. And that is what frightens us so.

Later we saw you sitting in the courtroom with members of the Hawkins crowd. Of course they are your friends and your kinfolk. And of course you are a fine self-respecting woman who runs the best restaurant in town and who has slaved at your business to earn the money to put your children through college.

Just as Lincoln Steffens said long ago, it is respectable people like you, who keep your own hands clean, yet rationalize the transgressions of those to whom you are in some way beholden, who are the warp or the woof of every corrupt power structure in America.

The Establishment came to America with the colonists. In New England it was the theocracy; in the southern colonies, the land-owners. But always there have been favors for the privileged and rewards for those who could grant them.

There is always a way to handle a man who gets out of line, a lynching, a barn burning, a foreclosure, loss of a job—a term in the penitentiary.

Things are bad in Morrilton for Gene Wirges and his friends. Yet is there a community in America about which it may be said, "It can't happen here?"—H.R.L.

From Knitting to News in Morrilton, Arkansas

Kenneth Starck

Two years have elapsed since that night of terror on the streets of Morrilton, Arkansas, but Betty Wirges talks about it as though it happened last night.

Her husband, Eugene, former editor-publisher of the *Morrilton Democrat,* a weekly newspaper engaged in a vise-tight struggle with the city's political rulers, had been arrested on a charge of contempt of court and locked in the third-floor jailhouse of the Conway County Courthouse in Morrilton. The jail's other five occupants, being held on charges ranging from criminal assault to drunkenness, had been removed.

The newspaperman was alone. "We were concerned about Gene's safety," recalls Mrs. Wirges. "We wondered whether he would walk out of that jail again. No one was allowed to see him.

"To make sure he was all right, we had agreed that periodically at night I would shine a spotlight on his cell window. That was to be a signal for him to appear, and then we'd know he was all right.

"One of those nights I remember I was out by the car. It was dark and windy. The trees and leaves and bushes were moving in the wind. And then, suddenly, it looked like the swaying limbs and bushes were people. And they seemed to be fighting. I panicked.

Reprinted from *Grassroots Editor* 7, no. 3 (July 1966): 10–11.

"I went home and called an attorney, and he quieted me down. It's the only time I've panicked."

One panic in two years—that isn't a bad record for a weekly newspaper editor. For it was in the summer of 1964 that Mrs. Wirges took over her husband's unbelievable chair as editor of the *Democrat*. During the past two years this blonde, gray-eyed, thirty-eight-year-old mother of five—who would rather stay home and knit—has occupied the hot seat in the newspaper's relentless battle against an acknowledged political machine that has controlled this picturesque Ozark county for more than two decades.

"It came as a surprise when they asked me to edit the paper," says Mrs. Wirges, whose only newspaper experience had included helping her husband and a two-week stint as editor when the newspaper was sold to friendly creditors. "But I didn't hesitate. I jumped at the chance. It meant we could operate the paper as we had before."

Mrs. Wirges was asked to become editor by a group of local businessmen who formed Conway County Press, Inc., in 1964, and bought the newspaper from friendly creditors in Little Rock. The Wirgeses had lost the newspaper following a series of clashes with the county political organization.

"We felt that if Gene were to come back as editor," said Mrs. Wirges, "that they [the political organization], would be able to drum up more indictments.

Indeed, her husband's legal battles read like a law textbook. Since the newspaper became involved in the struggle in 1960, Conway County juries have returned two libel judgments against Mr. Wirges for a total of $275,000 and convicted him of perjury. One libel judgment was overturned, the other dismissed with prejudice. The perjury conviction, which brought a sentence of three years in prison, took place February 3 and is being appealed. He still faces two other indictments—one for slander and another for conspiracy to have the county sheriff falsely arrested.

After nearly two years in her position, Mrs. Wirges has learned that weekly editor has the right to echo the same sentiments of the housewife who says her work is never done.

Her work week usually spans the seven days. A typical week's schedule: Monday and Tuesday, 8:30 A.M. to about 12:00 P.M.,

Wednesday, 8:30 A.M. to 8:00 P.M.; Thursday and Friday 8:30 A.M. to 5:00 P.M.; Saturday and Sunday, sporadic, as duties dictate. Assisting with the production of the offset weekly are six other employees, including two part-time students, and Mr. Wirges.

Mrs. Wirges's duties ran the gamut of weekly newspapers. Selling and laying out ads. Editing. Writing heads. Reporting. Writing editorials. Laying out news and editorial pages. Sometimes snapping photos. (Son—Ronald, seventeen, handles darkroom work.) Helping bundle papers for mailing. And the multitude of other tasks that go with the calling.

"Some people," says Mrs. Wirges, "come in and ask me 'What are you getting out of this?' That makes me madder than anything. My response is that there are a few people—and I'm sorry you're not one of them—who think we should be able to hand on to the next generation their individual freedoms."

And for a mother, there are other problems. "Recently, our six-year-old [the children: Ronald, seventeen; Victoria, fifteen; Gregory, nine; Michélle, six; and George, three] visited another little girl in the neighborhood, and Michélle was asked if she knew her daddy had been in jail. Of course, she wanted to know why, just like all the children do when they see Gene on TV. It's hard to explain to children. What do you tell them? The only satisfaction that I'll get from this job is to see all this [the county political situation] cleaned up so that this is a good place to live—not only for our five children—but for all the children in the community."

The best part of her editor's job, she says, is meeting people. The most disagreeable: Being away from her family. Too, there is a certain frustration—inherent in any weekly editor's job—of not being able to help everyone who needs help.

"People bring in their problems. They have an illness in the family and can't get help. Or they've been taken off the welfare rolls for not supporting the [county] administration. At one point I tried to help them. But there are just too many. Another thing I don't like is bringing up this political situation over and over again. I wish all we had to write about was something good. I've never had anything to do with newspapering other than criticism. And I've got the strictest critic in the world myself. Yes, my husband."

But that works both ways. "A lot of his stories I'll read and say, 'No, they [the readers] won't understand this.' He'll do the same for me. They say if two people are married long enough, they begin to look alike. The same maybe applies to writing. Both of us get depressed at times. Fortunately not at the same time. Often one of us has thrown up his hands and said, 'Why? Why?' And the other one is always there to answer why."

Of course, there are incidents that brighten a weekly newspaper editor's day. Recently a Morrilton youth wrote to the newspaper from South Vietnam inquiring about the price of a subscription. "We decided to send him a free subscription, and we offered to send to all of our Conway County boys overseas free subscriptions."

Has Mrs. Wirges encountered any personal attacks or abuse similar to that of her husband, who, besides being jailed for four days in 1964, over the years has been threatened and assaulted?

"There's been some. But not much. People, I think are a little reluctant to attack a mother of five. Once the sheriff's wife called. [Sheriff Marlin Hawkins is considered the leader of the county political organization.] He had been in a car accident, and she said, 'We'll take care of you if anything other than the truth is printed.' I said, 'We'll print the truth as well as your threat.' And we did. Our only protection is to make these things public."

How about social activities? "A lot of clubs and organizations were so intermingled [in membership] that I resigned from everything to avoid embarrassing anyone. We had even stayed away from church for awhile because of what was being said. But that was only for awhile. We've picked up where we had left off. And I'm thankful for that." (The Wirges are members of Sacred Heart Church in Morrilton.)

The past six years have been trying times for the Wirgeses. Maybe it would be easier for them to leave the town of six thousand to its own destiny. "If you run once," is the firm reply of Mrs. Wirges, "where will you run the next time? If Gene had quit, I just don't think I could have respected him."

As for herself, Mrs. Wirges leaves no doubt about her eagerness to give up her role as weekly editor and return to the role of housewife. When will that be?

"I think when we get a change in government, a change in courts and a change in the jury system. It looks good this year. The state will have a new governor, and several of the long-time officeholders in the county stand a good chance of being voted out. When that happens, I'll gladly relinquish the paper. And then I can pick up my knitting where I left it."

More about the Mighty Mice

■ Editor J. A. Newborn, Jr., of the *Suburban Journal,* Clear Lake City, Texas, is built just right to play tight end for the Houston Colts. He knocked around all over the world in a lot of interesting jobs and he proved himself to be quite a man. But he hadn't seen anything until he undertook to operate his own newspaper.

After a quiet beginning things began to warm up. What looked like hanky-panky in the business affairs of the local schools led into a bit of investigative reporting. A popular administrator was confronted with evidence of kickback, arranged through a friendly bank, from a salesman representing a firm which makes and sells high school rings. The whole town went on its ear. The Rotarians gave Newborn the boot for reporting unfavorably about a fellow member. Some of the advertisers pulled out of the paper. There were the usual threats and a few broken windows, plus a half-million-dollar libel suit.

But Editor Newborn stood his ground, finally counterattacked with a campaign for new faces on the school board and won. Yes, he is quite a man. In a few words this is why J. A. Newborn, Jr., was selected to receive the 1967 Elijah Parish Lovejoy Award for Courage in Journalism.

Editor Newborn reached for the plaque—for the first time in his life became speechless. When he regained his composure, he remarked, "I didn't expect to get a trophy from Balfour."

Just because he wrote an editorial against killing people, Alvin J. Remmenga, of the *Cloverdale* (Calif.) *Reveille* became the most unpopular man in town. Editor Remmenga's editorial headed, "Killing for Kicks," was a protest against capital punishment which called upon Governor Reagan and the people of California to halt the slaughter of sixty men waiting in death row.

Reprinted from *Grassroots Editor* 8, no. 5 (September–October 1967): 2–3.

Editor-without-portfolio Eugene Wirges, who still identifies with the *Morrilton* (Ark.) *Democrat,* although the paper was foreclosed by friendly creditors and turned over to the editorship of his wife Betty, is not going to have to chop cotton for three years on the Arkansas Prison Farm. The state supreme court set aside the verdict and sentence railroaded through Conway County Circuit Court, and Wirges at last is free of a long series of criminal harrassments at the hands of county politicians.

Now Sheriff Marlin Hawkins is under indictment. The mastermind of the Conway County machine, who controlled the elections by intimidating live voters and voting dead ones in the absentee boxes, will find it necessary to explain to a judge a few things about the disposition of fees and fines collected in the astronomical number of traffic convictions rolled up during the twelve years of his regime.

Editor J. R. Freeman may not last out the year as proprietor of the *Farmer and Miner* of Frederick, Colorado, but his pebbles cast into a murky pool may yet produce a wave strong enough to engulf the private interests seeking legalistic ways to steal from the American people the priceless resources represented in federally owned oil shale lands.

Freeman has been hounded, shot at, and traduced, but he continues to put in a full workweek on his investigations of irregularities in the handling of oil shale land in addition to mechanical work on his newspaper.

Freeman's address before members of St. Louis area Sigma Delta Chi chapters and participants in the International Conference of Weekly Newspaper Editors session was a stirring appeal for help in his work to expose the oil shale grab "not from any other individual nor other group, but help only from among my fellow newspapermen." His story of hardship and indifference was sad enough to cause a lobbyist to weep.

Ironically enough, just as Freeman approaches the breaking point, the press and public leaders are beginning to heed his plea.

Another editor whose contribution to the exposure of the oil shale scandal should not be minimized is Eugene Cervi, whose *Rocky Mountain Journal* of Denver long has spoken out in favor of retaining the oil shale reserves in the public domain. A recent issue of *Cervi's Journal* contained four articles on this subject, one of which revealed that the cost of extracting the oil would amount to only some thirty cents a barrel instead of a previously quoted figure almost as great as the value of the oil.

Cervi, who has more causes than all of King Arthur's lads, unhorsed another set of adversaries recently when he appeared in Washington as a witness against the so-called failing newspaper legislation under review in the Senate Judiciary Subcommittee. Gene's colorful presentation and his pungent replies to unfriendly questions are reported to have made shambles of the hearing as long as he was in the room.

Truly it was the Mighty Mice who scored heavily against the move to legalize unfair business practices of giant corporations in competition with smaller and weaker competitors. Except for the work of Stuart Paddock, of the Paddock Publications, Arlington Heights, Illinois, S.1312 might well have been heard in committee without a semblance of organized opposition. It was Paddock who hired lawyers, put in motion a fund-raising campaign and set up a corporation to administer the funds. It was Paddock who found the delegates at the meeting, in Richmond, of the National Newspaper Association wholly uninformed about S.1312 and set in motion a low-key campaign which on the final day of the convention produced a resolution in opposition to granting monopolistic privileges to metropolitan newspapers.

Hazel Brannon Smith, *Lexington* (Miss.) *Advertiser,* was forced to interrupt her campaign for election to the state senate to clean up the mess after a fire, apparently of incendiary origin, crippled her newspaper plant. In a small edition printed on a jobber while her large press was undergoing repairs, Hazel editorialized that she could not believe that any resident of her home county had been guilty of setting fire to her newspaper building. Hazel who holds such honors as the Elijah Parish Lovejoy Award for Courage in Journalism, the Golden Quill Award for Editorial Writing and the Pulitzer Prize was among the finalists in the Golden Quill Contest again this year on the subject of school burning in Louisiana.

And so goes the work of the Mighty Mice—H.R.L.

Weekly Editor Campaigns against "Giveaway"

Clifton O. Lawhorne

An all-out campaign to prevent what he calls a federal "giveaway" of some billions of dollars in future oil shale revenues from public lands is currently being conducted by Editor J. R. Freeman of the weekly *Farmer and Miner* in Frederick, Colorado.

His contention is that the U.S. Department of Interior, in effect trustee of the lands for the public, is standing by while big oil companies and speculators acquire the oil shale lands from the government for $2.50 an acre while the over-the-counter worth is $2,000 an acre.

Some six million acres of shale lands lie in Colorado, Utah and Wyoming in the public domain, and Freeman cites Interior Department figures to the effect that these lands have shale oil deposits totaling possibly eight trillion barrels.

Further, Freeman cites figures to the effect that many of the individual acres of the land contain nearly four million barrels of oil. If only 25 percent of it could be recovered, an acre could produce $2.5 million worth of marketable crude (at $2.50 a barrel). He contends that with Colorado oil shale lands developed in public ownership, the federal government would be assured of a royalty of $312,500 an acre, of which Colorado would get $117,000. The people of the United States will get only $1,600 a section at the "giveaway" price of $2.50 an acre, he points out. The hitch, however, is that so far no marketable method of surfacing the crude has been found.

But even as the situation is, Freeman points out that if a speculator can buy a section (640 acres) of such land from Uncle Sam, he can make a million bucks right off. This is by parlaying the $2.50-an-acre purchase into a $2,000-an-acre sale. It appears, he has written, that some 100,000 acres of shale oil land has been disposed of on the $2.50-an-acre basis in the last fifteen or twenty

Reprinted from *Grassroots Editor* 7, no. 4 (October 1966): 19–20.

years. More than 380,000 acres of the oil shale land in Colorado are now in private ownership.

Freeman fears more of it will end up that way as a result of old oil shale mining claims filed forty-six years or more ago. Current speculators are using these old claims to make demands for purchase of the acreage. An Interior Department official testified in 1965 before the Senate Committee on Interior and Insular Affairs that 300 such claims covering 50,000 acres were then actively before the department. It is estimated the old claims, numbering from 15,000 to 150,000, involve from 1.5 to 4.5 million acres of the Colorado land, a large part of that in the public domain.

Currently thirteen lawsuits are pending in the Federal District Court at Denver in which an effort is being made to overrule the Interior Department's decision that the old claims are invalid.

Freeman, in a series of articles starting in May, suggests that the oil shale lands should be developed by an agency like the Tennessee Valley Authority to provide the public with its ultimate interest.

He points to Senate Bill 2708 introduced by Sen. Paul H. Douglas which would use the oil shale revenues to pay off the national debt. But he also points to Senate Bill 1009 sponsored by Sen. Gordon Allott of Colorado for a complete relinquishing at $2.50 an acre of thousands of acres of the valuable oil shale lands. Freeman calls this Allott's "giveaway bill."

At least two other weekly newspapers have carried Freeman's articles—the *Midlothian* (Tex.) *Mirror* and *Manhattan East* of New York. The series has prompted *Manhattan East* to ask "Who's playing the shell game?" The New York newspaper also has quoted a "close observer" as saying the question involving public interest "is going to make Teapot Dome look like a Sunday School picnic."

Freeman in his series states that a substantial number of former federal employees who worked on oil shale disposals or development for the Interior Department and other agencies are now actual applicants for large acreages of such land "on the basis of phony pre-1920 mining claims."

"The potentiality of becoming an 'instant millionaire' by converting an 'investment' of a couple of thousand dollars into a multi-million dollar return has apparently created a situation heavily wrought with temptation," he writes. Freeman has called for a full public disclosure of "the roles, positions and financial or employment connections of the employees and officials in the executive branch and in the Congress who have been approving claims or making legal or policy decisions relating to oil shale land."

In doing so he claims the Department of Interior is now saying that many of the old mining claims, once declared null and void, are really valid and binding. He states that Frank J. Berry, solicitor of the Interior Department, on July 30 last year reversed old "null and void" decisions in contested cases on such flimsy grounds that, in one instance, the claimant did not have proper notice since his wife signed a receipt for a registered letter.

Freeman also states that the Colorado legislature in 1964 sneaked two provisions, one in committee, on a tax bill that exempted oil shale from severance taxes and provided a 274 percent depletion allowance. He said this was a "giveaway" of benefits that would have accrued to the people of Colorado. At the time it was passed, Freeman says *Cervi's Rocky Mountain Journal* in Denver could find only one formal entity in the state that seemed to know about the sneaker.

The Freeman series has been sent to congressmen, and Colorado congressman, Wayne Aspinal, wrote Freeman several letters taking exception to the "giveaway" designation. He said he was fully in support of the development of the oil shale industry but at the same time wanted to be sure the people of Colorado and America derive full benefit from them. "I see no reason why we cannot move toward the full development of this valuable natural resource without jeopardizing the interest of the public," Aspinal wrote.

However Freeman states Aspinal would not provide him with answers to a number of questions on the basis it would cost several millions of dollars to conduct the ambitious research project. He writes that Aspinal is widely quoted as a leading exponent of leasing and turning the oil shale lands to private interests.

Further complicating the picture, according to Freeman, is the new exploration of the lands allowed since 1964, leading to the discovery of dawsonite, a compound of sodium and aluminum.

The *Denver Post* reported recently that since March 31, some 2,750 mining claims have been filed on dawsonite discoveries. Also on July 28 the *St. Louis Post-Dispatch* reported that in a three-

month period ending July 8 some 3,225 dawsonite claims were
filed in Colorado on the oil shale lands.

The dawsonite issue is the "modern day equivalent of the Trojan
Horse," Freeman claims. "We feel sure that its chief value is acting
as a blind or cover for the special interest to steal the oil shale
from the public."

Freeman has been especially critical of Secretary of Interior
Stewart Udall and John A. Carver, Jr., the undersecretary. Carver
also has been queried by Freeman. But his answer to Freeman,
as published in the series, stated that "your questions would require
a heavy burden of research and voluminous exposition."

Carver also said: "Your concern appears to revolve primarily
around the validity of private claims to the oil shale resource. That
issue is in process of adjudication in the federal courts, where it
belongs, and all resources of this department and the Department
of Justice have been committed to protection of the public interest
in the litigation. I have ultimate confidence in the ability of our
judiciary to do justice under the law applicable to these claims."

However Freeman states that "the real danger is that the giveaway
minded Interior Department under the leadership of Stewart
Udall and John Carver, pusher by the unseen hands of bands of
congressmen and senators that are controlled by the grabbing
interests, might find just enough color in these [dawsonite] claims
to turn publicly-owned lands containing the vast stock of oil in
the oil shale over to the big oil and mineral companies before
the oil shale is developed and before the general public knows
the facts about its true astronomic value."

$4 Trillion in the Kitty

Blair Macy

We talked about it again at the newspaper conference in Illinois
last week. But now, following deeper investigation, the estimated

First published in the *Windsor* (Colo.) *Beacon*. Reprinted from *Grassroots Editor*
7, no. 4 (October 1966): 18.

total value being discussed is $4 trillion ("trillion," not "billion").

This is the value of the shale oil land so desperately wanted by leading American oil companies, who don't wish to develop it yet, for thirty or forty years. (They pressured Eisenhower to close the research plant at Rifle, as I recall. It remained closed ten years.)

But the oil companies certainly want the leases—cheap. They aren't advertising—"Wanted, shale oil land." They're more guileful. Sneaky, you might say.

How do they do it? Since the "Teapot Dome" scandal in 1920, it's been harder. But not impossible, evidently.

Colorado senators Dominick and Allott have proposed Senate Bill 1009, letting the oil companies have the oil shale under the pretext of "developing Colorado's resources." Aspinal, at the head of the House interior committee, will play an important role.

Palmer Burch, statehouse politician, sneaked a sentence into another Colorado bill in 1964—hardly any of the state legislators were aware of it. It offers a depletion allowance to the oil companies working shale oil "to show Washington." Allott and Dominick later explained, "that Coloradoans want the oil companies to get this tax deduction." ("What Coloradoans?" we might ask.)

So far I've heard no Colorado politician say he thinks oil companies get more than a fair share for exploiting a natural resource, or that he as a legislator is acting to curb any recurrence of a "Teapot Dome" scandal.

Until one does so declare, we can only assume that all our Colorado politicians are scrambling to outdo one another in "earning" financial support from the wealthy oil industry.

Who's on the people's side? There's a Senate investigation committee working on it, but every committee in Washington probably has a few members already on the oil industry's "gift list."

Both the *Denver Post* and the *Rocky Mountain News* have reporters capable of investigating this matter without disrupting the daily routine of publication, but neither seems concerned.

So we're down to a single little weekly editor, J. R. Freeman of Frederick, who's devoting almost forty hours a week trying to ferret out who's giving away how much to whom for what.

A lot of politicians are gambling heavily that it won't be, but if this shale oil thing is eventually exposed as a huge example of political cumshaw, then the Denver dailies will have sold out their illustrious heritage for—whatever they are getting.

Also among the list of those who were derelict in their duties will be the *Greeley Tribune,* the *Fort Collins Coloradoan,* and the *Loveland Reporter,* all of whom could play an important role in this matter.

We Windsorites can't do much about it, except keep our eyes open. It is really an exciting drama being run from week to week in the *Frederick Farmer and Miner* and you might like to keep up to date on this battle between an elephant and a mouse. The cost of the Frederick paper is only $3.50 a year.

If someday soon this matter comes to light, and political conniving is revealed, obviously someone bigger than Freeman will take over the investigation and get all the credit for exposing it.

But of this I am now convinced: Freeman is not trying to make a mountain out of a molehill. There is a great and sometimes dishonest effort being made by oil speculators to "steal" shale oil from an unsuspecting public. The oil companies do want it kept hush-hush, and Colorado politicians ARE playing hard, and for keeps, to help them get away with it.

A Courageous Editor

Houstoun Waring

The press of Colorado should pursue the shooting of Editor J. R. Freeman until the would-be-murder is solved. The case may be too big for the Weld County sheriff, and Colorado does not yet have its crime detection agency in operation.

On the morning of May 8, Editor Freeman was driving from his office at the *Frederick Farmer and Miner* to Boulder. About six miles west of Frederick, on Colorado Highway 52, he was fired upon by someone in a blue Oldsmobile. One bullet broke the

First published in the *Littleton* (Colo.) *Independent.* Reprinted from *Grassroots Editor* 9, no. 4 (July–August 1968): 12.

window behind him and showered glass down his neck. All bullets hit the 1961 International Scout in which he was traveling to Boulder.

After the third bullet, the editor was able to turn off the highway and run into the O. J. Nichols farm where he called the sheriff and the state patrol.

It would seem that officers could have sounded an alarm for all blue Oldsmobiles in a fifty mile radius, but twenty-four days have passed and no arrests have been made.

This lack of concern by Colorado newspapers and law officers reminds us of the Lucero case a generation ago. Editor Lucero was publishing a newspaper in Jefferson County, using it to attack gamblers. One gambler paid some arsonists to destroy the newspaper plant.

The incident failed to arouse the Colorado press, just as the present shooting has. This is incomprehensible. In the case of Editor Freeman, the assault occurred while he was en route to the university to confer with two professors in regard to the oil shale controversy.

The Frederick newspaper has done more than any other to alert the nation about the possibility of a giveaway in this natural resource—valuable enough to pay off the national debt. Mr. Freeman supplied *Ramparts* magazine with data for its last issue, and soon after publication the shooting took place.

Ramparts sees a possible connection between the attack and oil shale. It reports that other opponents of the giveaway have been intimidated. It does not seem likely that great corporations would resort to such tactics, but many greedy individuals are after those shale lands and some of them may not be too scrupulous.

We know the history of J. R. Freeman. He was working on the *Dallas Morning News* three years ago when he heard Penn Jones, a Texas editor, give a stirring speech at the Unitarian church. Mr. Jones urged his listeners to get into action and wage a battle for the common man—the American people. Mr. Freeman resigned his lucrative job and bought the Frederick paper which he operates with his beautiful wife, Elaine.

Editor Freeman rolled up his sleeves and began operating in the public interest. He has made enemies besides the oil shale crowd. His telephone has been tapped, his desk has been rifled, and he has suffered financially. One night he was trailed back to town by a car. He tried slowing down and speeding up. He went up alleys and through side streets. Driving into his yard, he hurried to call the town marshal. This earlier scare had a happy ending; the man trailing him had been ordered to repossess a mortgaged car—one that resembled the editor's.

The West seldom boasts an editor as courageous as Mr. Freeman has proven himself to be. In late years, this breed has mostly found roots in the South. Editors in other states have expressed their concern about the May 8 shooting. It is the duty of Colorado journalism to see that the case is solved.

Tennessee Weekly Editor Arouses Nest of Hornets

Dean Ribuffoni

The paragraphs which I have written today, and into whose cold sentences your masterly hand has infused the fervent spirit of Tennessee journalism, will wake up another nest of hornets—Associate editor to chief editor, from "Journalism in Tennessee" by Mark Twain. First published in the *Buffalo Express,* September 4, 1869

Mark Twain's one-hundred-year-old short story about journalism in the Volunteer State is a humorous one: the story of a newly arrived newspaper editor who finds Tennessee journalism to be "too stirring for me," and who is shot at, beaten up by strangers, and "scared to death" by "all the blackguards in the country."

Twain's 1869 story is, of course, fiction. But there is a very similar story of Tennessee journalism which is not fiction: it's the 1969 story of Dan Hicks, Jr., a Tennessee editor who has been shot

Reprinted from *Grassroots Editor* 10, no. 5 (September–October 1969): 13–15.

at, beaten up by strangers, and "scared to death" by people who could well be described as "blackguards."

Hicks, forty-seven, is the editor and part owner of the *Monroe County Democrat,* a weekly newspaper published in Madisonville, Tennessee. Madisonville, located in the foothills of the Great Smoky Mountains about forty miles southwest of Knoxville, is, in Hicks's words, "short on industry, education, and culture." But the community is also Hicks's home, and the city in which he is determined to make "good, meaningful change."

A tall, tousle-haired, bespectacled man with a sense of humor—a humor not unlike Mark Twain's—Hicks describes himself, in a voice with a crisp Appalachian twang, as an "editor-crusader."

And an editor-crusader is just what Hicks is, and he has performed admirably, against formidable obstacles, in his self-chosen role. He has waged a continual war against what he considers to be evils and wrongs, and he has won and lost battles which only the press can fight—and which only the press can win or lose.

How well he has performed can be illustrated by the fact that he was recently honored with two coveted awards: the thirteenth annual Elijah Parish Lovejoy Award for Courage in Journalism, presented by the Department of Journalism, Southern Illinois University, and the 1969 Golden Quill Award for Editorial Writing by the International Conference of Weekly Newspaper Editors.

The winning of the two awards by Hicks marked the first time an editor has won both prizes in the same year. The individual judges of the two competitions were unaware that the winner they had chosen also was the recipient of the other award.

Dan Hicks's career as an editor-crusader began long before his international recognition came. It began in the offices of the *Monroe County Democrat,* but when the weekly publication had a different editor-owner.

That editor-owner was Dan Hicks's father, a man who crusaded, according to his son, "against the boll weevil, for motherhood and the flag—and he had a lot of people who agreed with him."

His son had a different idea of what "crusading" was, however, and he decided to practice it somewhat differently. He had some excellent tutors, having worked for eighteen years on other newspapers, including those in nearby Knoxville and Norfolk, Virginia.

One of his employers and tutors was Horace V. Wells, Jr., president of the *Clinton Courier News* and himself a past recipient of the Lovejoy Award for Courage in Journalism.

Hicks credits Wells with teaching him "to tell it like it is." And when he returned to his hometown of Madisonville and to the *Monroe County Democrat* in August, 1967, Hicks was a man determined to "tell it like it is" at any price.

What Hicks returned home to was an eight-page newspaper with a weekly circulation of about two thousand copies. Today it's a sixteen-page weekly publication with a circulation of over six thousand copies, an increase largely due to Hicks's journalistic knowhow and his spectacular crusading efforts.

His crusading began somewhat unspectacularly, with editorials against what he considered to be racy movie advertisements and the ungentlemanly behavior of adults at local athletic events. He rapidly expanded his efforts, however, with criticism of the labor unions which were creating havoc in Monroe County. Hicks fought for new industry in the area, and against the union-inspired violence which had caused one manufacturing plant to close and others to threaten to do so.

Then he argued against the secret meetings of elected public officials which were being held in the county; fought to get a new courthouse for the county, disclosing dangerous structural weaknesses in the dilapidated edifice; and wrote editorials concerning abuses in the Medicare administration for the Madisonville area.

And he continued to expand his one-man crusade, creating new battle fronts for the weekly newspaper: an investigation into Madisonville's inadequate water system; exposure of the Ku Klux Klan's intimidation of Negroes and other minority groups in Monroe County; a vigorous campaign for qualified persons to run for the county school board; the uncovering of a large amount of evidence of misconduct and illegal activities by the Monroe County road superintendent; a fight for relocation of the city's sanitary landfill; a campaign to provide up-to-date equipment for the county's rescue squad.

And much, much more. Hicks's endeavors spread to every corner of Monroe County, and his crusade continually, took on new issues and opponents.

What Hicks received for his indefatigable efforts was little more than public apathy, however.

"I had expected a goodly part of the good people in Monroe County to back me up in public; to support these good causes," Hicks said. "But I couldn't get the people worked up." In truth, however, he did get some people "worked up": those individuals to whom the label "blackguards" might have been applied by Mark Twain.

While he expanded his crusade, Hicks began to receive warnings from various "concerned individuals" that he was "pushing too hard" and "rocking the boat." The warnings were soon replaced by threatening telephone calls and obscene letters to the Tennessee editor.

In September, 1968, following his investigation into the abuses of public funds by the Monroe County Road Department, Hicks found himself the victim of physical assault: he was beaten by two teen-age boys, hired by a local bootlegger who had been selling illegal liquor to county employees.

In the same month, two shotgun blasts were fired into the *Democrat* office while Hicks was inside working, narrowly missing him. The men who fired the blasts were former employees of the Road Department.

In October, 1968, a second shotgun blast was fired into Hicks's newspaper office by an unknown person or persons. In November, 1968, his newspaper plant was robbed of fifteen-hundred-dollars-worth of camera equipment and office machines. The robber was not caught, nor were the valuables recovered.

The "fervent spirit of Tennessee journalism" that Mark Twain had written about continued to push Hicks, however, despite the assault, attacks, and threats. He now carried a gun around for protection and continued to publish his paper. His attackers were apprehended and prosecuted by the law, although Hicks says that "I still have more than my share of enemies 'on the loose.' "

Despite the public apathy to his campaigns and the personal assaults, Hicks did get satisfaction into seeing slow but meaningful change come to Monroe County: Madisonville's water system has been updated; one KKK organizer left the city under pressure from Hicks's disclosure of Klan activities; the Monroe County

School Board has gained new, qualified individuals—individuals Hicks feels are worthy of their responsible positions; the Monroe County road superintendent resigned under Hicks's editorial pressure and grand jury indictment; the county's rescue squad has gained new equipment.

And perhaps just as important a change has occurred in the newspaper readers in Monroe County. In Hicks's words, "Today it matters what the *Monroe County Democrat* says. Back in August, 1967, when we first started publishing, it didn't make a difference. But today it does. Every newspaper in Tennessee runs a tremendous amount of linage on 'freedom of the press,' but we don't have freedom of the press. Tennessee is a backward state in many ways, but if every newspaper in the state did what I'm doing, we'd truly progress."

Today despite the journalistic honors he has received for his crusading efforts, and the changes he has brought to Madisonville and Monroe County, Hicks still regards his task as being far from finished. "I've only gotten into a small, small part of what has to be done, the Tennessee editor said. "The question is: Do I have enough years left to help right what is wrong?"

Perhaps Hicks doesn't have enough years left: his task is an arduous one, and one which would doubtlessly tax the abilities of a dozen good editor-crusaders. But he has taken the first steps and he has done so in an atmosphere hardly conducive to journalistic crusading.

One hundred years ago, Mark Twain wrote: "Tennessean journalism is too stirring for me." In 1969, Dan Hicks, Jr., is finding that Tennesseean journalism is not too stirring for him.

Monroe Placed under
Moral Indictment
by Shot Fired into Negro Home

Dan Hicks, Jr.

The citizens of Monroe County and Madisonville were morally indicted by the three shots which were fired into the Madisonville home of a Negro leader, early Sunday. But for the grace of God, one of the bullets would certainly have struck and killed an innocent sleeping five-year-old boy who doesn't even know what the terms integration and civil rights mean.

Had the youth been killed, the crime would have been as heinous as the murder of Sen. Robert Kennedy which occurred less than a week earlier because both incidents were hate inspired. The lessons which should have been learned from the murder of Kennedy are all too slow to penetrate into the minds of some Monroe County people.

The responsible citizens of the area can thank God that the bullet missed the child, because if it had killed him, the name of Madisonville would have been added to that of Clinton, Dallas, Memphis, and Los Angeles.

The moral indictment further charges the people of this area with going to church and listening to the teachings of the greatest lover of his fellowman and then going out to practice hate the rest of the week, teaching their children to hate by putting pressure on their pastors and teachers to not preach and teach the brotherhood of man and of being complacent and of refusing to be involved.

So far this month, crosses have been burned in front of both a white and a colored church, a windshield has been shot out of a car, two Ku Klux Klan rallies have been held and a Negro home has been struck with bullets. What will it take to wake up the citizens of the Madisonville area and cause them to take immediate

---

First published in the *Monroe County Democrat* (Madisonville, Tenn.) Reprinted from *Grassroots Editor* 10, no. 5 (September–October 1969): 12, 27.

action to prevent incidents that could be even more tragic?

We were impressed by the number of our nation's leaders—the president, congressmen, police officials, and ministers—who took to the air following the assassination of Kennedy to urge the people to abide by the law and to urge the law enforcement officers to enforce the laws. They all agreed that the breakdown in law enforcement has been responsible for the murder of President John F. Kennedy, Dr. Martin Luther King, and last week of Sen. R. F. Kennedy.

But the pleas of these leaders glanced off the minds of the officials and citizens of Monroe County and Madisonville. We say this because three people were stopped near the scene of the cross-burning at the Negro church, their whiskey was poured out and they were permitted to go on their way.

When three men were stopped after the Negro house had been struck with bullets, they were not even arrested for questioning. And a governmental official who witnessed a law violation refused to testify against the violator because he does business with him.

The citizens of this area must rise up and demand that their elected officials impose a crackdown on law violation, if the present lawless trend is to be reversed and peace restored here.

The pastors of the churches must stand in their pulpits and preach the teachings of Jesus Christ concerning brotherly love, in spite of the wishes of their congregations.

The teachers in the schools must stand in front of their students and teach the principles of true democracy, without being afraid of the school patrons and officials.

The community leaders must demand that hatemongers like George Myers, Ku Klux Klan leader, be controlled. And somehow we must organize and present a solid front to stem the growing wave of race incidents here.

One leader, when we told him of the shooting, said, "If Black had kept his mouth shut his house would not have been shot into." We are dumbfounded because we thought everyone in this nation believed in freedom of speech. At least everyone says he does.

Another leader said, "I was telling someone last night that they ought to go over in the Park and shoot up Black's home." The shoe would have been on the other foot if three Negroes had shot the speaker's home because of his inflammatory statement.

"I cannot bring myself to believe that the majority of the people in Madisonville do not look with disfavor on shooting into homes and the burning of crosses and that they want it stopped," the wife of a pastor stated. Could she be wrong?

Every reader of this newspaper, in his own heart, knows that God loves that little five-year-old Negro boy as much or more than he does the most influential rich man in Monroe County. If they do not, then we are lost.

And the editor of this newspaper knows full well that should he or his loved ones be shot in their home some of the community leaders would say, "if he had kept his mouth shut, it would not have happened." But, by keeping their own mouths shut they are giving away their own rights and freedoms and it just might be their homes which are fired into next.

It's no use, Monroe County, you cannot close your eyes and have it go away. You will be involved, one way or the other, whether you want to or not! For if you do not go to the fight, the fight will come to you!

Tell It Like It Is

Baxter Melton

In March, 1954, Ro Gardner arrived in Hickman, Kentucky, to edit and publish the weekly *Hickman Courier* and to report the news as he saw it. Sixteen years later—in March, 1970—Gardner and his family had to leave Hickman because he did that job too well.

Specifically, Gardner had to sell his newspaper and move on because of an advertising boycott by local merchants. The boycott was in answer to Gardner's factual reporting and editorializing on racial issues at the Fulton County High School in Hickman.

Fighting for black rights was something unacceptable to most whites who total 80 percent of the thirty-seven-hundred population

Reprinted from *Grassroots Editor* 11, no. 5 (September–October 1970): 7–10.

in the county-seat Mississippi River community. Gardner, then thirty, and his wife Lee, bought the ninety-five-year-old *Courier* in southwestern Kentucky after looking at other weeklies in the Midwest and his native Mississippi.

Under Gardner's ownership, the *Courier* won state and national awards, and was instrumental in Hickman's acquiring its own water, gas, and electric systems, this bringing to Hickman the Graphite Division of Carborundum Company and also a two-hundred-thousand-dollar grant for the Port of Hickman Authority.

His fearless type of old-time crusading dates back to his first year in the community, when he editorialized on "Backwoods Justice." This editorial was about a woman accused of murdering her husband. The case was delayed years until there were no witnesses, then it was dismissed. Yet three destitute teen-agers, according to the editorial, got two years each in the state penitentiary for stealing hogs.

Gardner also ruffled the local Establishment from the first with his idea that "as long as you fear to reach out and annex areas, this town will never grow." Also, he said editorially, farmers living just outside the city limits enjoyed all the city benefits without paying for them. Areas were annexed as a result of this stand.

His first fight with the school board also came that first year—resulting from alleged brutality to a ten-year-old black student. "The superintendent later showed me the two-ply strap the teacher had used, after some school authorities previously had vigorously denied and implied in unison that the child had been whipped with a bare hand," he has said.

Gardner was no newcomer in the most recent racial situation that led to his leaving Hickman; he also had upheld other Constitutional rights in situations involving people or his newspaper. In 1959, he won a Freedom of Information case in circuit court for access to the county's fine ledger. In this, he brought legal action against the county judge, whom Gardner had supported for election because the man was a lawyer, and Gardner thought the county judge should be a lawyer. Then the judge closed the fine ledger to the Hickman paper while allowing it to be examined by any other paper.

The judge's reason? Editorial comment by Gardner that "they

need revolving doors at the county jail, the way they have so many prisoners in and out of there so often." But it was the continuing racial issue at the local school which brought everything to a climax for Gardner—admittedly a crusader "and never a middleground for me."

Six months of racial strife at FCHS, and the series of events destined to end in the advertising boycott, began on Monday, October 30, 1969. The first incident was a confrontation between a white male teacher and a black female student. The *Courier* reported that the twenty-four-year-old teacher admittedly came to school mad that morning, "sure that black students had kicked in the fenders of his sports car Friday night while he was chaperoning a high school dance." It was later proved, however, that two white boys had done the damage.

A week later, the *Courier* reported that a black male student had been suspended because he had gone to the defense of the black girl. The boy also was removed from the Student Council, which voted three to two to keep him on. But the principal vetoed this action.

"Racial Roulette?" was the heading on Editor Gardner's plain-talk editorial that week: "We can learn something from it . . . we champion neither the students nor their teacher. . . . Both were wrong . . . American people are on trial now, and we have a chance in this community to prove that at least here in Hickman, we can measure up to those opportunities . . . treat each other decently and accept the fact that the War Between the States was over some 104 years ago . . . a chance to set a rather excellent Christian example for the nation."

After that, things got worse instead of better. The school board did appoint a black teacher from grade school as an assistant basketball coach, after a committee of aggrieved black students and parents appeared before the board to protest racial discrimination. And Gardner ran, in nearly a full-page article in the next issue, the list of Negro school grievances presented to the board.

Physical troubles at FCHS did not occur again until January, some two months after the first incident. Then there was a confrontation between the principal and black students at the January 10 homecoming event. After two blacks repeatedly refused to take off their hats and sunglasses, or to leave the gym, the principal knocked off one's hat and glasses.

Black students felt that a ten-day suspension for the two students involved, plus banishment from all extracurricular activities for the remainder of the year and corporal punishment upon their return, was unusually severe penance. The principal refused to have a student assembly to air grievances. "The black students just want to make more speeches," the *Courier* story quoted the principal.

Then followed an intensive nine-week period of letters to the editor, with black students supporting the editor who maintained the rights of blacks "to be human beings," and white students and teachers protesting that Gardner was "damaging the community by his interference and destructive criticism of the educational system."

The January 15 publication date of the *Courier* is believed to have marked the start of the underground boycott of the paper by white citizens. These people threatened local and area merchants with the loss of their business, "if you continue to advertise in the *Courier*."

"To my amazement," Gardner recalls, "I watched advertising drop week by week until I had only a 46 percent average in a ten-page tabloid, compared to over 60 percent previously in a fourteen-page issue."

In his January 29 issue, responding to constant criticism, Gardner's editorial was headed "Advice to Hypocrites: If You Don't Like It, Don't Buy It!" He had been printing unfavorable letters as well as those backing him. And this was his answer to some of these letters and other attacks:

"If the shoe fits, wear it . . . let's quit playing games with each other in Hickman. Which is to say, quit using the *Courier*, its editor, his wife and his children as scapegoats every time something unpleasant happens in his community and is reported in this paper. If you don't like it, don't buy it. If you don't like living where a newspaper may express its honest opinions of matters of importance to the community, then we suggest you move. . . . As long as we run a newspaper, we are going to report the news—tell it like it is—and give you our unashamed opinion of things we deem important to the upbringing of this community. This serves as a fair warning also to those who have been making calls in the middle of the night—which do more to scare hell out of the editor's kids than to get even with the editor."

He then pointed out that a telephone device, requested of the company, would aid in apprehending and convicting those who made these calls. "Perhaps we will be brought screaming into the present century . . . it is time for the people of this town to wake up out of their 100-year reverie and recognize that it is no longer true the White is right and Black—solely because of its color—is wrong."

On February 2, the principal evicted twenty-three students—seven whites and sixteen blacks—on a newly enacted rule on shaving. The Negroes included most of the black male seniors. Editor Gardner promptly labeled this as "a ridiculous charade" and added that "until a change of principal and principles at the high school, the problem is going to get worse." The principal was not reemployed in that position for the 1970-71 year. He was transferred to a lesser role in a county school.

In the February 5 issue, a five-by-seven-inch picture of a fourteen-year-old black dismissed for not shaving was printed alongside Gardner's editorial, headed "Close Shave." The close-up showed barely a suggestion of hair—on the student's upper lip.

Meanwhile, the Kentucky Human Rights Commission and federal investigators from the U.S. Department of Health, Education, and Welfare had been called in when the black parents and students could make no progress with school officials.

The Kentucky Civil Liberties Union entered the situation as legal counsel for the black parents and students. A temporary injunction was sought to readmit ousted students without prejudice, while merits of the case were tried. Specifically, KCLU would seek to prove the right to grow moustaches and beards as a personal freedom guaranteed by the Constitution. A December 1969 Wisconsin precedent in the U.S. Supreme Court, involving a high school student's right to wear long hair, was used.

But still there was no dialogue between the Hickman whites and blacks. The white community became more entrenched. Black parents and students sought a return to school and formation of a biracial committee to handle any differences that would come up in the future.

On the advice of a Kentucky Department of Education investigator, who said he could find no evidence of racial discrimination, school authorities staged what Gardner described as a "so-called public meeting at which only school authorities would read from prepared texts." The meeting, said his editorial, was "a whitewash" which "sought to defend anything the school had done and to deny the pleas of black students and parents."

The closest thing to support for Gardner from the white sector of Hickman was a letter from a regular churchgoer, who wrote, "It is our Christian duty to love our neighbors as ourselves." But over a hundred letters from a dozen other states and many phone calls buoyed the hopes of the editor, his wife, and their children.

In a house advertisement, the *Courier* told advertisers that it did not seek approval of its editorial policy when soliciting ads. The *Courier* wanted "only to be considered as sales medium . . . and this is a free country." But Gardner said he and his wife wondered if, in reality, a newspaper, "was free to report unpleasant news, as well as social chit-chat and service-club boosterism."

When he asked advertisers if they really were participating in a boycott, "Some frankly admitted it. Others played games with me, or finally broke down and admitted fear of losing business if they continued to advertise with me. I was alternately frightened and mad as hell," he recalls. "What kind of country is this that we can let people tell us when, where, or with whom we can advertise, because of the almighty dollar? I didn't know, as an editor who'd never kissed anyone's backside, the problems of maintaining a retail personality. Like the bank president had said, 'I don't give a damn about what anybody thinks,' so full speed ahead."

Things began to happen when KCLU filed its suit at the beginning of the sixth month of racial differences and the eighth straight week of front-page news about black and white difficulties. First newspaper support for Gardner came from western Kentucky's biggest daily, the *Paducah Sun-Democrat*. In a final editorial paragraph about Editor Dan Hicks's situation in Madisonville, Tennessee, and his sleeping with a gun at his side because of fearless reporting, the *Sun-Democrat* noted: "Ro Gardner, at Hickman, knows exactly how it feels to be intimidated for exercising his right of free speech. Boycotts, as well as direct physical retaliation, are forms of intimidations of newspapers that amount to suppression of thought as well as speech."

This *Sun-Democrat* editorial item was followed by an advertisement from a biracial committee in nearby Fulton, the more urban of Fulton County's two communities. The committee urged "moral and financial support of the *Hickman Courier.*"

Ironically, Fulton's daily newspaper accepted an opportunity to aid the boycott. Advertisements dropped from the *Courier* began to appear in a free-circulation shopper printed by the daily and distributed in Hickman. The *Fulton County News*, a weekly, refused to print the shopper for ethical reasons. Louisville's *Courier-Journal*, Kentucky's largest newspaper, headed a lengthy article, including pictures, with "A Kentuckian's Costly Fight to Print the News."

Gardner said he wondered, at times, if physical violence might not be better than the kind of boycott in effect. His wife got to the point where she did not want to go out in town, "there was so much hate in people's eyes." A child told Robin, the Gardners' twelve-year-old daughter, that "I'm glad Ro Gardner is not my daddy." And Hickman residents, especially merchants, were quoted as saying, "We'd be better off without him." A letter writer suggested that he "leave the banks of this Mississippi River town quietly and unobserved."

But not everybody in Hickman wanted the Gardners to leave. This was especially true of the town's black population—about 10 percent of its residents. "He's the champion of the oppressed," said P. L. Nichols, a black man. "He has told it straight, and the Establishment doesn't like it." Nichols, who has the respect of many blacks and whites, is assistant to the elementary school principal.

Advertisements of support were run by the Black Parent-Student Committee, paid for by many small contributions and aimed at keeping the *Courier* alive and hopefully getting their message across to the white community.

Meanwhile, the *Courier* called a kind of editorial truce in the eighth week of ever-increasing hate. "Since the matter now is in the hands of the courts and HEW, further debate on the editorial page of this newspaper would be an exercise in futility and an endurance contest in bitterness," Gardner wrote.

The problem seemed resolved, a week later, when the Federal

judge for Kentucky's Western District ordered black students back
into school temporarily. He offered the school community a chance
to work out the differences back home. But black students were
back in school only three days before the board announced new
disciplinary rules and regulations. The personal appearance code
was invokved again, also the moustache and beard rule, as well
as the ban against extremely long hair—this against the advice of
the board's attorney.

If students did not comply, the principal said, "no use to come
back to school." Nine students, facing suspension, appealed. In
federal district court, the judge upheld the school, citing that the
matter was being confused with "black power," rather than the
original context of moustache and hair rules. The *Courier*, the
KCLU, and the state Human Rights Commission continued to
support the black students.

But the *Courier* advertising lineage continued to decrease.
Gardner wanted to continue the fight, to sell his car or anything
else, but because of his wife and children, decided to leave. On
March 28, the Gardners sold the *Courier* "at a reasonable price"
to Paul and Jo Westpheling, owners of the weekly *Fulton County
News*. The *Courier* now is printed in the Fulton plant. Mrs. Westpheling, its editor, goes daily to the Hickman office.

The Westphelings announced that they would put out the kind
of paper the Hickman people apparently wanted. It would be, they
said, a chronicle of events and include school, church, and social
items. "We plan no editorials at present, except the front-page
personal column type," they promised.

Gardner, one of weekly newspapers' "last angry men," went to
Montgomery, West Virginia, where he is public information officer
for the Montgomery General Hospital.

"A combination of being able to write, to take pictures, and
to tell the hospital story honestly to the community provides me
with some satisfaction. My future possibly will be on a college
campus teaching reporting and news photography, if I am fortunate
enough to find a place where I feel at home where freedom is
concerned," Gardner said.

"As for Hickman's future," Gardner added, "I feel what happened when we were there cannot be erased. The town sooner

or later will have to face the fact that rural ghettos exist as surely as those in Watts or Harlem. The old magnolia-scented notions can never be as fragrant as they once were in the future of emerging citizenship for minorities."

Bessie Stagg: Case Study in Advocacy Journalism

■ More than anything else, events of the last decade should have reminded us that in a country with no licensing of journalists, the public interest frequently is best served by those least qualified by wealth, education, or professional status.

For example there is Bessie Stagg, editor and publisher of the *Bartonville* (Ill.) *News*, whose involvements in local issues, so turgid as to defy the comprehension of a stranger, have kept her in hot water for months on end. Her concern was for such matters as closed meeting policies of the local school board and alleged fiscal irregularities by the township board. Because Bartonville is a small community in which the people are more at home with informal practices than they are with the niceties of procedure, personality conflicts blur the apparent facts and at times themselves become the issue.

Mrs. Stagg had no journalistic training or experience. In fact she became an editor simply by setting up shop with a typewriter on her kitchen table. At the time, the community had no newspaper. Public officials of the various local agencies had come to look upon the business of the schools and other government operated enterprises as their own private preserves. Perhaps because there was no medium for public accounting, they can be excused for drifting into this attitude. Nevertheless, the people talked, as they usually do when kept in the dark. Because Mrs. Stagg was an energetic person with a concern for events and because her husband worked in the production department of a daily newspaper, Bessie was urged by her friends to start a newspaper. If nothing else, this was a democratic approach to the problem of communication at the grass roots.

Reprinted from *Grassroots Editor* 13. no. 3 (May–June 1972): 2–3. 10.

Bessie's ability to spell and to write good sentences did not match the quality of her intentions or the intensity of her zeal. To the thoughtless, her little, homemade sheet with its jagged lines, crooked pasteup, typographical errors, and stylistic aberrations was a joke. But it was no joke to Bessie Stagg that patrons of the schools were unhappy, that when she sought information from the public record, she was turned aside as a meddling busybody. Bessie, as much as any editor who has ever lived in America, had a mission. In the face of hatred, ridicule, and contempt, Mrs. Stagg continued to wrangle with her detractors, always seeming to come a little bit closer to information the people in power were determined to keep hidden from the public. Finally the *Bartonville News* was able to produce evidence of irregularities in the records of Limestone Township of sufficient magnitude to create a scandal of the first degree.

After standing aloof through much of the conflict, even at times permitting reporters to make light of Mrs. Stagg and her newspaper, the *Peoria Journal Star* presented editorially this handsome appraisal:

> A probe of the Limestone township books by the office of the attorney general of Illinois is welcome news. We have had a look at them and we can't make any more sense of them than Bessie Stagg, *Bartonville News* publisher and editor, could.
>
> In addition the fiery editor from Bartonville advises us that a variety of activities and statements were put in her path to avoid the plain legal obligation of ready access to public records.
>
> That is always suspicious, and the fact that officialdom there "doesn't like" Bessie is no excuse. What they like least, obviously, is her constant probing.
>
> We also have reason to suspect that Limestone is not alone, but that town funds are peculiarly susceptible these days to irregularities, and therefore, a thorough probe in Limestone may produce benefits far beyond the boundaries of that township alone.
>
> We predict that Bessie Stagg's latest tempest will end in some new legislation in Springfield that is badly needed, be-

cause as things now stand it is very difficult indeed to have an effective accountability and monitoring of how townships handle their funds.

In that long and agonized stretch of time between her first kitchen-table editorial and this accolade by the leading newspaper of her area, Mrs. Stagg, by her own account, suffered the following retaliations: a libel suit for one million dollars, establishment of a rival newspaper, threatening letters and telephone calls, withdrawal of legal printing by local officials, mistreatment of her children at school, pressure upon her advertisers to discontinue their patronage, an attempt by the driver of a bulldozer to push her and her car into the city dump, wave after wave of slanderous stories, dismissal from membership in the Illinois Press Association.

One can forgive local people for their excesses in the heat of emotional confrontation. After all, Bessie handles herself rather well in a fight and she gave as good as she took. But if Bessie was kicked out of the Illinois Press Association for publishing a lousy newspaper, it is time to admit that the First Amendment applies equally to Bessie Stagg, the little sheet set up to put her out of business, and the greatest newspaper in the state of Illinois. Most appropriate is an apology to Bessie, restoration to membership, and serious consideration for the Editor of the Year Award in 1973. Bessie is a lady and she will forgive.

With or without sanction of professional peers Bessie Stagg has made a place for herself in that company of bright spirits and brave souls enumerated as the heroes and heroines of the American Press.

It is true that the meek shall inherit the earth, but only as legatees of those who raise hell.—H.R.L.

Anyone for a Fight?

Jack Fought

She may be the Midwest's fightingest weekly editor, but she would
deny the label. Yet within recent months Mrs. Bessie Stagg, editor
and publisher of the *Bartonville* (Ill.) *News* has been sued for $1
million by a real estate developer; successfully campaigned against
a local dump operator; exposed misuses of funds in a high school
work program; repeatedly brought about improvements in her
community by revealing unhealthy or dangerous situations; withstood an attempt to drive her out of business through an advertising
boycott.

Furthermore, she keeps right on fighting what she sees as wrongdoing, although at times she flirts with the thought of giving up.
Whenever she nearly reaches that decision, a new cause develops,
and Bessie Stagg is its champion. "I don't want to be destructive,
unnecessarily," says the housewife-turned-editor and Bartonville's
best-known resident, "But I'm trying to point out to the people
how much power they have."

From a journalistic point of view, her attempts to instruct readers
in this regard might be considered unorthodox. The *Bartonville
News* is not a typical weekly operation. It was founded, according
to Bessie, after she was told to do so by an inner voice nearly
fourteen years ago. "I knew Bartonville needed a newspaper," she
said, "and if it was going to get one, I'd have to do it."

The *News* was the village's first newspaper in its fifty-five-year
history, Bessie said. The fact that she had no experience on a
newspaper and had never been trained in journalism did not deter
her in her mission. With less than one hundred dollars in cash
and a borrowed typewriter, she started putting together the first
issue of the *News* in her home in Bartonville, a suburb of Peoria
in north central Illinois. Her home still serves as the newspaper
office.

Her unprofessional approach may have been partly responsible
for what success she has enjoyed. The *News* is folksy in appearance
and content. She is clearly a crusader and it shows in routine news

Reprinted from *Grassroots Editor* 12, no. 1 (January–February 1971): 17–19.

coverage. Under a page-1 headline reading "Teachers Get Hefty Pay Raise," she wrote:

"The Bartonville School teachers were evidently given a hefty raise this year. Who told us this? We learned it from three local citizens. Whether this information is 100% correct cannot be stated. We should not have to get our information from a citizen, who is not connected with the school, but that we did. Since it seems we cannot do anything about these secret meetings we shall stick our proverbial neck out, and tell you what we heard. We feel the people who pay the bill should know what is going on, so here goes."

And often she takes her readers into her confidence. In her column called "Buzzin' Bessie" during the investigation of a school official, she told her readers:

"About four o'clock Sunday evening we retreated from everyone and asked God to direct us further. We had about come to the end of our understanding. We were told by God, in his way, the next person that came into our office we should give them the problem. . . . Bless my husband, he cooked, cleaned house while I was so busy and he really made the biggest sacrifice when he didn't go fishing and leave me alone. Now that is love."

Husband Bill is a pressman for the Peoria *Journal Star.* Although he occasionally "goes out to pick up ads when someone calls in," he takes no direct hand in the operation or direction of his wife's newspaper.

Bessie is assisted part-time by a woman who collects personal briefs, but Bessie herself writes and edits the eight-page tabloid. It is printed by offset at Astoria, Illinois. She admits that the *News* could not survive if she depended on advertising revenue and subscriptions at three dollars a year. Paid advertising may total only 25 percent of a typical issue.

On the other hand, she says she has never solicited advertising, and to her knowledge she has lost only one advertiser because of an editorial stand. Not long ago, however, the Limestone Community High School Board voted to deny her newspaper advertising in hopes that she would go out of business. The board president was quoted in a news story as referring to her as "a detriment to the community."

She has complained about a lack of support from Peoria area
newsmen and the Illinois Press Association, of which she had been
a member for a number of years, did not invite her to reaffiliate
for 1971.

The Bartonville School Board has also criticized her and her
reporting. "With but few exceptions, The *Bartonville News* is, from
cover to cover, nothing more than the editorial opinion of one
person, its publisher-editor-owner," the board declared in a sixty-
column-inch letter to the editor which she printed. Bessie had
charged that teachers at the Bartonville grade school beat children
and that board members met secretly to conduct business.

"If the Board had something other than a biased, prejudiced,
totally one-sided newspaper to turn to that would print the 'facts'
and 'figures' (instead of just the sole, often uneducated, uninformed
opinion of one person) these allegations could each be reasonably
defended," the board responded.

Attorneys for both the high school and the grade school boards
have threatened lawsuits although none has developed. Individual
board members have taken action on their own, however. One
grade school board member, who was also a mailman, refused
to deliver her newspapers during a two-year hassle, Bessie said,
but she ultimately prevailed.

Bartonville's mayor, Gerald Stuaan has offered some praise for
the embattled editor. They get along well, he has said, because
he gives her the information she is entitled to. Stuaan credits her
with helping in numerous community projects and for her sincere
interest in youth.

Bessie appears to have an uncanny nose for news. When she
gets on to a story, no matter how faint the trail, her prey is soon
at bay. "You're not able to hide anything from her," Mayor Stuaan
says.

Recently, when she heard that a teacher at Limestone High had,
perhaps jokingly, suggested that students should toss a bomb at
the *News*, Bessie methodically tracked down the source of the
statement and got the police chief to issue a stern warning to the
person involved.

Bessie contends that she has only community welfare in mind
in her skirmishes with her antagonists. Apart from her role as editor,

she is also a housewife and mother. Two of her sons graduated from local schools and a daughter is still in high school.

Partly as a result of her long-standing feud with the school boards, which she has accused repeatedly of questionable practices and violating the Illinois open meeting law, she has been denied access to board meetings. This has placed her in the role of underdog, and consequently the number of news tips have increased sharply.

She says she averages eight tips a day, mostly from persons who want her to fight a battle for them. Her usual reply is to ask what the caller intends to do for himself, and she gives advice on where he may obtain help to relieve his problem. Not infrequently, however, if she gets two or more calls on the same issue, she will print the complaint without comment. Ordinarily the situation is remedied shortly thereafter.

When one resident, after complaining for four years about some rat-infested, junked school buses in violation of zoning ordinances, sought her help, Bessie simply ran a picture of the buses and the woman's statement in the cutline. Town officials chided Bessie for her approach—but eliminated the problem nevertheless.

Bessie says her paper serves as a deterrent factor. The fear of seeing the situation exposed in her newspaper serves to keep potential wrongdoers more honest, she feels. Although she never endorses a candidate in her newspaper, she is often consulted on political matters.

It was Bessie's boldness that led to the $1 million libel suit filed by a real estate developer. Bessie contended in print that the developer changed the date of his application to get under the deadline for newer and stricter road and gutter regulations. The suit was never brought to trial.

The same openness caused her to criticize a dump operator who, she declared, was polluting a creek that runs through Bartonville. While in her car taking pictures on the dump site she was threatened by dump workers, who smashed a garbage truck into her automobile and considered tossing her car, with Bessie and her son Tom inside, to the bottom of the dump. She had the ultimate satisfaction, however, of seeing the dump operator fined five thousand dollars and his dump operation cleaned up.

An earthy woman whose language leaves no doubt as to its

meaning, Bessie at the same time is religious in her own way and regularly seeks divine guidance. She is indignant when she sees children mistreated or if she thinks a story will hurt someone. For this reason she does not mention suicide in obituaries. "I always ask myself, 'Is it going to hurt a young person?' I'm not news crazy, and I would prefer to help someone even if it means I won't get the story."

Her desire to help youngsters got her involved in the story about the misuse of federal work program funds by an official at Limestone High School. The official, who admitted using a student for baby-sitting in his home and paying her with federal funds, subsequently resigned. "I did it for the student's sake," Bessie told her readers. "I have never seen her, but she is God's child, she was made in his Image and Likeness and as the Bible states we have to love one another."

Bessie's *Bartonville News* may never be on firm ground financially, but that is not her concern. She says she has had several opportunities to sell but has declined the offers because of the enjoyment she gets out of newspapering.

Although her newspaper reaches, by her own estimate, only about seventeen hundred homes, she is not concerned with the relatively small circulation. For the past two years she has experienced severe competition from a local shopper with greater circulation. "I don't believe in numbers but in the success of the publication," Bessie says. "A small town paper that knows the people can do better than a large paper to serve the people," she adds.

But doesn't serving the people lead inevitably to clashes? She admits it does but insists that she tempers her responses, even when she is in her fightingest moods. "I don't try to get even," she says. "That would be revenge. But I'll give them praise if they back down and straighten up."

Gish

Edmund B. Lambeth

At Mrs. Siller Brown's in Ice, Kentucky, hospitality is a sprout of ginseng herb for your ulcer and a glass of well water on the porch. At Arthur Dixon's in Whitesburg, it's the cool of the cellar workshop, where, surrounded by handcrafted clocks, dulcimers, and rifles, you can hear a mountain man tell it like it was. At Mrs. Alma Whitaker's in Roxana, news is a vigorous bean patch and surprise visitors from Morristown, Tennessee.

In person and in print, Siller, Arthur, and Alma are doing what has come naturally to generations of country correspondents. Yet their folk news keeps company with some of the most inspired hell-raising in American journalism. They are participants in the *Whitesburg* ("It Screams") *Mountain Eagle,* edited and published by Tom Gish and his wife, Pat. At circulation thirty-seven hundred, theirs is one of the most influential newspapers not only in Kentucky but Appalachia as well.

Among several hundred subscribers outside Kentucky are some two hundred in Washington, D.C.—chiefly bureaucrats, lawmakers, and professional Appalachia watchers who have been educated to respect the *Eagle* as an authentic regional voice. Others of these *Eagle* loyalists include admiring journalists, mountain historians, Kentuckians in urban Diaspora, plus a number of nameless Middle Americans who simply yearn for their vanished sense of community.

Typical of the latter is a Mrs. Beulah Monroe of Lyons, Oregon, who wrote Gish about what the *Eagle* did for her: "Even though I am a stranger I feel after reading it that I've had a good visit with friends." Or Elaine Griffin of Green Bay, Wisconsin: "I feel I know joys and feel sad when the news is sorrowful."

Thousands of others know Tom Gish's Appalachia through Letcher County's more famous son, Harry Caudill, whose *Night Comes to the Cumberlands* is credited with first putting the region on the IOU list of elected politicians. As close friends, Caudill and Gish have fought together against the entrenched, absentee mining interests that both men see as having raped the mountains

Reprinted from *Grassroots Editor* 12, no. 1 (January-February 1971): 17-19.

of their beauty, wealth, and health. While many newspapers looked the other way at the plunder, Gish and his wife Pat have relentlessly pursued the strip miners, photographing and reporting the pollution and ugliness left behind and exposing the plight of those left to live near the hazards of strip mine spoil banks. Gish's stories have named names and placed blame, as a result of which, according to Caudill: "It's a thousand wonders he hasn't been killed or had his house blown up. There are so few like Tom who know and are willing to say there is an alternative to the status quo. But I think that in the near future Kentucky will impose a severance tax on the miners, with the proceeds funneled back to the areas mined. And when this tax comes it will be due in no small measure to the very, very few in Kentucky who stood up, like Tom."

Gish's judgment of the Appalachian Regional Commission (ARC) is linked to his crusade against strip mining. Says Gish editorially: "Eastern Kentucky might muddle through, somehow, with or without the RC, were it not for the total destruction that is being done by strip mining, which is destroying the mountains as a place to live as surely as an atomic explosion."

As for ARC's emphasis on roads, Gish thinks that in eastern Kentucky most of the new Appalachian highways are poorly designed and, in fact, unsafe. Recent accidents and growing complaints bolster his argument. As for ARCs' policy of concentrating aid in designated "urban growth centers," Gish contends that it bypasses the mountain poor. "ARC isn't a 'change' agency," says Gish. "It's run by some of the most conservative politicians in the country." For this kind of criticism, in the *Eagle* and in conversations with visiting newsmen, Gish was bounced from his position as "media representative" on the board of the Kentucky River Area Development District.

When Tom and Pat bought the *Eagle* in 1957, the local school superintendent and his board had conducted their business secretly for as long as anyone could remember. The Gishes successfully insisted on attending. They persistently publicized the school system's shortcomings, including an unsanitary cafeteria, exposed under the classic headline: "School Stinks." In 1964, bruised by the *Eagle*'s coverage, the school board withdrew its legal advertising from the paper—only to restore it after readers mounted a letter-writing campaign in the *Eagle*'s behalf. As a Whitesburg school official commented: "When Tom came to town the high school had twenty-seven faculty members. Now it has forty. Much of that is because of the agitation in his paper. And the school board sees its mission more clearly now, again because of Tom."

Not surprisingly, the Gishes pay for their independence. They are often ostracized and threatened. Advertising is withheld or minimized, as a result of which the Gishes make ends meet with the help of Pat's job as director of the Eastern Kentucky Housing Development Corp., a nonprofit antipoverty group. Recently, Hoover Dawahare, the largest merchandiser in eastern Kentucky, joined business hands with a right-wing editor, Charles Whitaker, publisher of a rival weekly with less than half the *Eagle*'s circulation. Yet Whitaker and Dawahare very nearly took from Gish his largest source of income—four thousand dollars in county legal notices. They did so by invoking an obscure statute requiring any paper receiving such notices to be printed within the county. This forced Gish to relocate his printing business from nearby Norton, Virginia, to Manchester, Kentucky, an extra three hours drive. Friends of Gish attribute the incident to powerful enemies in county government on the lookout for a chance to punish Gish.

Of how the *Eagle* came to be what it is, Gish responds with characteristic candor: "It would be romantic and nice if I could say Pat and I bought the paper to come up here and save eastern Kentucky. The fact is I had reported thirty-three sessions of the legislature for UPI and ten years was enough. The offer to buy this paper looked good. What we didn't know when we bought it was that the area had just reached the end of a boom. It hit bottom, real bottom. Practically every time I looked up there were people coming in the door begging. There was one old lady from Pikesville that just had to have three hundred dollars for an operation. I didn't have it. She later died. The accumulated problems of hunger and health were simply incredible. Harry [Caudill] and I just decided to use our previous contacts in the state and outside to stir up some interest."

In recent years the *Eagle* has been a harbor for young journalists eager to exercise their professional independence. Tom Bethell, a contributing editor of the *Washington Monthly,* gained material for a forthcoming book on the mining industry while volunteer reporting for the *Eagle*. Mike Clark, a conscientous objector assigned to Appalachia through the American Friends Service Committee, exposed in detail the destruction wrought by Beth-Elkhorn, a subsidiary of Bethlehem Steel, by strip mining in once beautiful Milstone Valley. "The present (Kentucky) law has not slowed down or hampered strip mining—despite loud cries of pain from the coal industry," Clark concluded. A young documentary photographer, Jean Martin Warholic, has published in the *Eagle* dozens of mountain life scenes (fiddling, hog-killing, herb-digging) rare for their honesty and in distinct contrast to the many condescending poverty portrayals of recent years.

"It is one of my constant sorrows," says Gish, "that I get about six requests for jobs each year that I have to turn down. I simply can't pay. It says a lot about the profession that it's so hard to find the kind of professional freedom they're seeking elsewhere."

Many of Gish's triumps—and a good deal of his suffering—stem from his unique posture in Appalachia as both a buffer against and a bridge to the Majority Culture. Homer Bigart, whose 1963 Appalachia story is credited with moving President Kennedy toward a war-on-poverty, is the most notable in a continuing stream of newsmen who touch base with Gish while covering Appalachia. Gish's ability to speak succinctly and colorfully about the region has won him a place in Bernard Birnhaum's *Christmas in Appalachia,* Eugene Jones's *Smalltown, USA,* and several others. Much of presidential candidate Robert Kennedy's visit to eastern Kentucky in 1968 was arranged by Gish. Pat Gish hopes to bring to Appalachia not only federal money but Ivy League architectural skill. His use of outside leverage has opened Gish to the inevitable charge of "running down his own town." Thus his right-wing rival culminates against the "damaging influence that liberal newsmakers have upon us when they come into eastern Kentucky to capitalize upon the helplessness of a few mountain families."

But Gish, a native son with a miner father and a deep sense of place, has intuitively negotiated with his readers, a subtle, unspoken agreement in which each allows the other to speak his mind. Correspondent Arthur Dixon's historical chronicles of the Regular Baptists of Letcher County are treated with as much deference as the *Washington Post* would show Walter Lippmann's memoirs. Lovers of Whitesburg have their say, but so do those who call attention, as one letter writer did, to the "beer and Clorox bottles and dead dogs floating down the river." The hell that Gish gives a local ARC official is reciprocated, *New York Times* style, with the official's full text reply. The ungrammatical spice in Siller Brown's lengthy report from Ice, Kentucky, is left to stand, not by calculation but for the *Eagle*'s unstudied preference for the natural. Gish's editorial genius is in striking this bargain with his readers while at the same time maintaining, unquestioned, his independence as arbiter of what to print.

Tom Gish laughingly recalls the time that Lyndon Johnson's speech writers cribbed from a national television documentary the comment that "when a small town dies a little bit of America dies." But like the small town, the *Eagle* is under the gun, too. And if despite Gish's own fortitude the *Eagle* should die, what can be said of American journalism?

Heroes, Living and Dead

■ When I think of Denver I think of journalism and many names I do not care to mention. When I think of the names I admire and respect I recall Eugene Field and Eugene Cervi.

Field and Cervi had so much in common. Both were little boys unwilling to abandon the whimsical delights of youth. Both enjoyed doing the things they had to do. Both were masters of their craft. Both contributed much to journalism and to Denver, their adopted city. Both were men of sorrows.

The contrasts were even greater. Field, the joyous prankster with no stomach for conflict, moved on to Chicago and to a professional environment suited to his tastes. Cervi made a calculated decision to remain in Denver and to serve as his own man, allied with, but never belonging to, the army of irregulars dedicated to keeping the Establishment from becoming too established.

In what started out as only a professional relationship I learned to love Gene Cervi as I love beer, dill pickles, country ham, grand opera, good ideas well expressed, and other joys of the flesh and the spirit best digested under rules of discretion.

Gene was with us in Carbondale less than a month before he died. Characteristically, he overstated his propositions, characteristically he challenged those who dissented. Characteristically he lost his cool. But when he made us uncomfortable, most of us loved it.

We spent an hour together having coffee and waiting for his plane. Gene said this would be his last campus visit and that never again would he undertake the ordeal of wrangling with students and faculty about the meaning of the role of the press in a predatory society.

We talked of our fathers and of our responses to youthful pres-

Reprinted from *Grassroots Editor* 12, no. 1 (January–February 1971): 2.

sures that had made rebels of us both. We talked of faith and the things we did not understand. We agreed that each man who is a man serves his faith in his own way without fear of the consequence. We talked of those who deceive the American public and we damned those who are aware, yet lend themselves to the conspiracy of silence.

We talked also of happier things: on the continued growth and development of *Cervi's Rocky Mountain Journal* and of the manner in which his daughter, Clé, was responding so ably to the challenge of editorship and management. Suddenly I remembered a book intended as a going away present, but left in my car. There was still time before he boarded to run to the parking lot and to make an inscription as I stood panting by the runway, I wrote:

To Gene Cervi
Denver's ombudsman and most demanding
self-critic.

"I like that," he said.

I wonder if he looked again on the plane. I wonder if he noticed the misspelled word. I wonder if he said, "Ignorant bastard!"

Eugene Sisto Cervi, born September 20, 1906, Centralia, Illinois, died December 15, 1970, Denver, Colorado. During his last visit at Southern Illinois University Gene Cervi spoke time and again of Bruce B. Brugmann, editor of the *San Francisco Bay Guardian,* as one of the great defenders of press freedom in America.

Brugmann's challenge in the courts, of the federal legislation relieving newspaper publishers, under certain conditions, of accountability required by the antitrust laws, was hailed by Cervi as one of the greatest contributions of the decade to freedom of the press. One of many Cervi questions: "Why have all the people in America who say they believe in press freedom left it up to the editor of a little newspaper out there in California to fight all by himself against monopoly ownership of the press?"

Reminded that Brugmann lacks the funds to keep his case alive in the courts, Gene responded, "I was a two-dollar bettor until the line became too long at that window, and I am a two-hundred dollar contributor to causes. I'll send Bruce a check as soon as I am back in Denver."

Whether or not Gene remembered to follow through on this impulse is not the point. The real point is that Gene Cervi respected Bruce Brugmann and was willing to support his cause. People have asked how they can honor the memory of Gene Cervi. The answer seems so obvious. Support Bruce Brugmann in the continuing fight against privilege. In memory of Gene Cervi send your check. The torch carried by Gene Cervi has been passed to all of us willing to keep the faith—H.R.L.

Confessions of a Failing Newspaper Editor

Bruce Brugmann

If members of Congress were really interested in a failing newspaper, they would come to me, and if they were interested in a failing publisher they would come to me. In the last five years I've lost about one hundred thousand dollars which I don't have. My wife and I have extended our credit and our relatives' credit and our Bank Americard credit and our Master Charge and so forth and so on the the point where there's no credit left.

Our newspaper, the *San Francisco Bay Guardian*, is not a weekly. We originally came out with the idea of being every other week. But we found out very quickly that we could not get the advertising because of the joint monopoly rate of the *San Francisco Examiner-Chronicle*. And many times we were lucky to come out only once a month. So I have a failing newspaper and I am a failing publisher, at least according to all the definitions I know anything about.

I like the *Grassroots Editor*. And, I like the fact that the School of Journalism at Southern Illinois University was about the only Journalism School in the country which I know anything about that had the guts and the audacity to put its professional academic prestige on the line and come out publicly and openly and directly against the Failing Newspaper Act or Newspaper Preservation Act,

Reprinted from *Grassroots Editor* 12, no. 4 (July–August 1971): 6–10.

which some have characterized very aptly as a mutual blackmail pact between the ANPA and the monopoly publishers and whatever government is in power.

I do feel a little bit humble being here tonight, particularly with a gentleman who has been run out of Kentucky and with the man who a couple of years ago was run out of Colorado on the oil shale issue. All that's really happened to me in San Francisco is that I've been banned from the Pulitzer Prize of the West Contest of the San Francisco Press Club, and that's just about as serious as it sounds. The background of this is very quickly: We had been doing a series of stories against P.G.&E., which is San Francisco's friendly private utility company you love to hate. San Francisco is one of the few cities in the United States that is required by law, by federal law, by U.S. Supreme Court decision, and by the city's own charter, to have public power. This is a result of a very interesting conservation decision which was made back in 1912. It allowed the city of San Francisco to go into Yosemite National Park and dam a beautiful valley to bring the water down to the city of San Francisco. In the process, the city was to get cheap electric power as well as the cheap water. The water got to San Francisco. The power never did. And the power never did because of a whole series of collusive arrangements between P.G.&E. and the city of San Francisco extending over a period of forty years. And it's such a hot issue that nobody in town will touch it except us. During the past two years, our stories, issue after issue, have hammered on this P.G.&E. story. Then a year ago June, the invitation for the Pulitzer of the West Contest came out for the Press Club. We were supposed to get one, but we didn't. I inquired as to why and was told to call the public relations man at P.G.&E., who was the head of the Pulitzer Prize Committee. So I called him up and asked why we were not able to be in the contest.

"Well," he said, "you know how it is. We wanted to encourage weeklies to get into the contest, and you're not a weekly. We felt that it would be better to encourage weeklies to get into the contest, and so you're not in this year." I asked if it had anything to do with the fact that he was the public relations man for P.G.&E. "Oh no, certainly not," he said. "No. No. In fact I resent the fact that you make this accusation. You're obviously an unobjective reporter."

In the next edition of the paper, we pinned a little medal on our masthead which said, "Banned by the San Francisco Press Club." And that's the story of how this particular issue worked. And this is, in many ways, how journalism works in San Francisco.

It might even be a first in American newspaper history, I don't know, but I have even been under surveillance by private detectives of the *San Francisco Chronicle*, which is the monopoly paper in town. It happened three years ago, when we began reviewing the public file of KRON at the time its license renewal came up. The *Chronicle* owns KRON, which is the major NBC radio affiliate and television subsidiary in San Francisco. I went into the *Chronicle* building, the KRON building, to check the public file to learn who actually owned the *Chronicle*. They have to put the names and addresses on file and give the exact percentages of ownership and all kinds of beneficial financial information that you get in no other way. As you know, newspapers don't have to divulge this sort of information. They only have to do it if they own a TV station or cable station, and they have to go before the FCC.

Anyway, ten minutes after I came out of the station, the station manager of KRON had called the station attorneys, who also represent the newspaper. Immediately private detectives were called, and my wife and I were under surveillance—so it turned out later during the KRON hearings—for a period of three to four months. They would wait outside of our house. When we left for the office, they would follow us. They followed me wherever I went. They even at one point sent a private detective into the office under the disguise of being a free-lance media man who wanted to do a report on San Francisco media. He interrogated me, the editor of a small little newspaper, supposedly for a series of stories. Along this line, we have filed a suit against the *Examiner-Chronicle* to invalidate the Failing Newspaper Act and in the process, hopefully, to invalidate all of the other twenty-one joint agency newspaper agreements in forty-two other cities where they exist.

This is a very difficult suit. After a year, I have only been able to raise fifteen hundred dollars. I have written most of the major publishers, business people in the media, journalism professors, and so forth; and I assure you that very few are interested in this kind of suit to the extent of giving my kind of money. We have gone through our first action in the U.S. District Court in San Francisco on the *Chronicle*'s motion to dismiss our suit. We have had oral arguments and it now rests with the Federal Judge Oliver Carter. He will decide in the next few weeks whether we have a trial in San Francisco and he upholds our contention that the suit is valid and should stay in federal court; or he upholds the *Chronicle* and it will be thrown out of court, whereby we will appeal. Both sides have announced that both sides intend to carry it to the U.S. Supreme Court as a First Amendment and Fifth Amendment due process test case.

The point I am kind of leading to here is that we are just a little paper. We don't come out very often, but we have still, I think, managed to get and to maintain a good deal of influence in San Francisco and maybe in the profession at large. Perhaps you can judge for yourself.

First of all, we criticize other newspapers and other radio stations and TV coverage in our stories. Most of you know that very few papers criticize each other. The big ones don't very much. And it is very interesting, of course, when you have two monopoly papers. The Ralph Nader Report came out on antitrust recently and gave extensive coverage to the Newspaper Preservation Act; the *San Francisco Examiner* merger in San Francisco in 1965 (nine months after the government filed the *Tucson* case); the politics behind the Salt Lake City merger; the politics with Representative Udall involving the *Tucson* case; a whole raft of good materials, particularly good stuff on L.A. and the very cozy merger agreement between the Hearst and Chandler interests in L.A. And I could find nothing anywhere in the press. The press does not like to get into these sorts of things.

So in our kinds of stories on the *Guardian* we are very interested in detailing exactly what the coverage is. How did TV cover it? How did the newspapers cover it? Why did the *Examiner-Chronicle* leave it out? Why was it or why wasn't it on television?

The reason for this is twofold. First of all, San Francisco is a press-conference town and everything is kind of scheduled. We are competing in what we call a kind of Haig and Haig journalism—journalism where the PR man comes into the Fairmont Hotel, slams down a bottle of Haig and Haig on the table, calls up the city editor of the *Chronicle* and the city editor of the *Examiner*, and a few assignment editors around town, and says, "I have a story over here, come on over." If there is nothing doing that day, the reporters come. And there is a story. If nobody comes and there was something doing that day, they'll just wait a couple of days and hold the same press conference all over again.

We also have to be careful of the corporate world. An example is the outlet Westinghouse owns, KPIX, which is our best and most outstanding television news operation in San Francisco. KPIX is operating in a joint venture with Dean & Dean, twenty miles down the coast of San Francisco in Half Moon Bay, and they are putting in this little fishing town a massive development of 120,000 people. And on the Half Moon Bay committee is a man from Dean & Dean and a man from Westinghouse. KPIX covers the event, goes down and does several nice stories on how Half Moon Bay is being cleaned up and how we ought to get behind this Half Moon Bay plan. Meanwhile, Westinghouse is developing plans to build a sewage treatment center by which they control all of the development in town and hold up the city council. Also, the city council and Westinghouse and Dean & Dean are all up in the legislature at Sacramento pushing a special bill that will release them from all controls on the coast side. The three forces are also opposing the conservation bill that would restrict the development.

Now you cannot do anything with this kind of a story, you see, until you get into all of the corporate connections—until you know what is going on in Sacramento—until you understand how KPIX is operating through Westinghouse to put this story in the best possible way.

Secondly, we do a good deal of investigative reporting in the Ralph Nader tradition. Actually we started doing this four or five years ago, before Nader really got going with his Nader's Raiders. We thoroughly investigate the air pollution and water pollution control district and we find out all of the industrial influence through the advisory committee, through the members on the board, and through the Bay Area League of Industrial Association. This is the association that up until about seven or eight months ago kept the district from releasing the figures of who were major polluters in the Bay Area.

Until we got going on this issue and a couple of citizens groups got into this—not radio, not television, not the daily papers, but us and a couple of citizens groups got into this—you didn't even know who the major polluters were in the Bay Area. And you didn't even know how much of the filth they were putting into the air and into the water each day by poundage. And you cannot do any kind of accountability or bring any polluter to task until you know publicly who he is, how much he puts into the air and water, and how he works politically with the proper government agency to reduce public pressure and to reduce public awareness.

We have done a whole series of things looking into the grand jury in San Francisco, and into the draft boards in San Francisco. And now, this summer, we have found that we still have much to do. Even though we aren't able to publish regularly, we file suit or something to give the idea that we are still in business. And we now have about seven attorneys working on various things offensively and defensively to keep us in business. We decided we have so much to do that we would set up four volunteer task forces working with the *Guardian* under our direction. We chose four specific areas.

One was the economics of high rise, which is exceedingly interesting and involves a lot of very sophisticated research and interdisciplinary work, checking city records and the whole business. What we found is that all of the elements that went into putting high rise and higher and higher densities and more and more traffic into Manhattan were being duplicated in the same kind of kamikaze development operation in San Francisco. And the development interests were poised to put the coup de grace on San Francisco this year.

There were about twenty-five major thirty- to fifty-story buildings coming into San Francisco. Plus, we found out on subsequent investigation that the chamber of commerce was putting together its own series of projects for San Francisco in which there would be clumps of high rises all over the city in almost every major area. And this beautiful, magnificent, great American city is going to be ruined within the next three to six years. What do you do?

What we're doing right now with this Nader's Raiders group is to try to determine how we can beat the businessman at his own game. What they do not get into is how much is the density going to cost. You have to build a rapid transit system for it; you have to put more cops on the corner; you have to have more elevator service. When you get a fire in a building that is thirty-five stories high, you have a hell of a time getting it out. What about welfare; what about buses?

In conjunction with this we have a second area for our Nader's Raiders—a coalition movement that's springing up now in San Francisco. It's a good coalition; it's a neighborhood coalition. It'll be an ethnically diverse, multiracial kind of commission. They're planning an initiative campaign against the high rise. They're going to try to take over the city and run a man against Mayor Alioto and run a man against the sheriff and run a man against the six incumbent supervisors and run a man for DA. The *Guardian*, as small as it is, has been providing editorial leadership on this project. We feel that it is our job to provide the editorial ammunition for this campaign. We're not going to get involved politically in the campaign. But we are going to provide the kind of hard, economic statistics we hope will neutralize and put the chamber real estate interests on the defensive for the first time in San Francisco.

Another Nader thing we're doing is—the third task force area we mapped out—is investigation every radio and television license in San Francisco. We're examining the public files, checking the programming, going over the public service announcements, who owns what, how many owners are out of town, and how many are in town, financial statements, time, news, and advertising matter, an whole series of things which can be done simply by inspecting the public files. In California the licenses are up September 1. We check now to see what was in the license three years ago—1968. September 1, we check again to see what they're proposing for this next year.

When we go into every station in town and say we're from the *Guardian*, we're checking your file, there is a very interesting thing that happens. It is very therapeutic, because three years ago we also were involved in the KRON case in which two challengers, with our help, challenged KRON's license. This kept the *Chronicle* from getting that license for the past three years, and has tied it up in FCC proceedings which has been very expensive. We will force them to divest themselves in their cable television operation. And we've forced them to change a lot of their news and editorial policies over this issue. This is just another example of the kind of influence a small newspaper can have.

And we think we've been extremely influential in our fourth "Nader Raider" area. Quite by accident last summer a young woman came into the office from the *Michigan State Daily*. She said she'd like to do some volunteer work. So I sent her out to break the codes in the supermarkets, the little codes on the cigarettes and eggs and the milk, and all the various items in the supermarket. Nobody had ever done this in California. It had been done kind of sporadically throughout the the country, but not on a really organized basis.

She spent two months breaking the codes in the supermarkets. She used various strategy, and sometimes she just asked the clerks directly. She broke most of the major codes, and we put them in the paper so that the housewife could take the section into the grocery store and figure out how fresh the food was. Now this is a very subversive thing to do, particularly if you have a lot of grocery ads. Of course, we're not about to get a lot of grocery ads. So we didn't have to worry about it. It's the kind of thing that none of the women's pages nor any of the news sections of any of the Bay Area papers had done.

As a result of this, the California Rural Legal Assistance Foundation (CRLA) came to us, took our material, and filed a suit against Borden's Milk, claiming the firm was discriminatory against elderly people. The elderly can only go out and shop once or twice every week or ten days. When they can't tell how fresh the milk is, they might have to return it. Or it might sour on them, and they might not be able to drink it, and they might lose some money. Or they might have to go back to the store. After the suit was filed, all of the milk outfits in California were open dating.

Then the CRLA attorney took the matter and our *Guardian* material to a southern California legislator and promoted an open food dating bill. There were hearings on it just two weeks ago, and it looks like we have a model open food dating bill in the state of California. Some of the legislators tell us it may be one of the best in the country from that kind of investigative story.

The point here, I think, from these various stories is that this is kind of a logical extension of adversary and investigative journalism—to do the story, then decide that disclosure is not enough, and then turn the material over to a congressman or a legislator who may move. In the case of P.G.&E., nobody in politics in the city of San Francisco is ever going to move without being clubbed daily for a long period of time. So, rather than wait for someone, we're soon getting ready to file suit against the secretary of interior to get him to force the city of San Francisco to start action for the first time in thirty years to buy out P.G.&E. There are about $40 million involved in lower utility rates, in cheaper power, and also more money for the general fund and possibly lower taxes in San Francisco.

We found that it's very effective to move into an advocacy position with our materials. It is a dangerous kind of thing to do. Once you start operating politically with your paper or yourself, trying to line up votes, trying to file suits, backing candidates in a very direct and personal way, you get into all of the normal hassles that come with politics. And you get identified with one group or another group. But nonetheless, I think, in certain strategic kinds of things, it really has to be done. And it can be done by the smaller papers. Sometimes a monopoly paper is not in the position to do it. And it shouldn't do it, simply because it is in a monopoly position. But a small paper can do this. A small paper can represent itself. A small paper can go down to the city council and argue. A small paper can file suits.

And just on the simple matter of information, we have a very difficult time, sometimes, in city hall getting information, particularly after they know that somebody's from the *Guardian*. We tell them we want to know who these guys are, now you tell us. If they don't we go to an attorney and try to get a writ of mandamus on the basis of this public information. And they have to prove on a statutory basis, on a very direct need-to-keep-secret basis that they can keep this information quiet. This is an extremely effective technique.

And the thing that bothers me as much as anything—the *Guardian* will survive—is that somehow there has to be a way for smaller papers and papers in trouble to get protection. There has to be a way for a small newspaper to get some legal help, to get a publicity man behind it at the right moment and to get the word out into the intellectual and political bloodstream of the larger regional or statewide area that the paper is in trouble; and that it's going to go down economically for this reason, or that reason, if it doesn't get an immediate transfusion of money.

And it seems to me that it's a very nice thing, that it's very important, to give an award to the man who's run out of Kentucky, and the man who's run out of Colorado, and to the man whose newspaper has been burned down after the fact. I think it's very nice and it's very important.

But I would just leave you with one thought. That is that perhaps out of the fund we're doing for the *Guardian*, which we call the fund for a free and competitive press, or perhaps out of the International Conference for Weekly Newspaper Editors, perhaps out of journalistic gatherings, there could be put together the machinery to go to the aid and succor of a paper that needs it.

Such machinery would have to have at its disposal a certain amount of money, say between fifty and one hundred thousand dollars, which perhaps could be raised from foundation sources or some of the sources which I tried to tap for the *Guardian* for my suit, it also would have attorneys available to it in specific areas of the country. We could bring in outside attorneys, some publicists, some advertising men, maybe some outside journalists, maybe even some men that are retired who could come in and give somebody a hand for a month. The problem I've found, when I'm really on the ropes, is that I'm just exhausted. And when it's a kind of a one-man or a man-and-wife or a small-family operation, you just don't have the energy and the time to fight these battles. That's why it would be good to have a roster of people who could come in and give you a hand.

Postcript: Why We Settled
Editorial in the San Francisco Bay Guardian *by Bruce B. Brugmann*

The *Bay Guardian* has accepted a $500,000 settlement to drop its antitrust lawsuit to break up the *Examiner-Chronicle* newspaper monopoly. The *Examiner* and *Chronicle* also paid an additional $850.000 to the owner of the defunct Weinstein's department store and to fifteen other plaintiffs in five related suits.

The case was settled on Friday, May 23; the trial was to begin on Tuesday, May 27. It had earlier been postponed a week by federal judge Oliver Carter. After paying attorneys' fees, the *Guardian*'s share will amount to about $300,000 before taxes. The settlement money will be used to pay back debts and to finance the switch this fall from fortnightly to weekly publication.

Additionally, the *Examiner* and *Chronicle* have agreed to negotiate with *Guardian* attorneys on access to the news vendors to see that the *Guardian* can be sold from the news huts on San Francisco streets. The street vendors are independent merchants (not employees of the two dailies), but the contract between the vendors union and the *Examiner-Chronicle* has been structured, the *Guardian* contends, to prevent or discourage them from selling other papers besides the dailies.

We decided to settle the suit with great reluctance and after much consideration. We still believe the *Examiner-Chronicle* joint operating agreement, which fixes advertising and circulation rates and pools profits, is illegal under the antitrust laws. We still believe that agreement is not exempted from the antitrust laws by that great publishers' plum, the Failing Newspaper Act, because the agreement killed a third newspaper, the *News Call-Bulletin,* because the preexisting papers were not in fact "failing" and because, among other reasons, the *Examiner* and *Chronicle* are in many ways not "independent" in their news and editorial policies.

We thought we could prove these things at trial, that we could break up the monopoly and ultimately invalidate the Failing Newspaper Act. But we found there's a limit to how far a small "failing newspaper" like the *Guardian* can go in fighting an antitrust case of this magnitude.

We found after five years of prosecuting this case that it was draining, and would continue seriously to drain for years, valuable money and energy away from the *Guardian.* It cost us $25,000 to $50,000 and several more years to fight the appeals all the way to the U.S. Supreme Court and to establish damages to the *Guardian* in a second trial. Moreover, there was no assurance that, even if we had won the case, we would get substantial damages.

So we settled out of court and got the money to do what we set out to do nine years ago: establish a first-rate competitive newspaper on a weekly basis. We're hopeful that, if the settlement strengthens the *Guardian* and its brand of journalism, it will do more in the short and long run for journalism in San Francisco than anything a lawsuit could have done to improve the *Examiner-Chronicle*.

Voice of the Little People

George M. Killenberg, Jr.

A remarkably sage, prophetic, and compassionate editorial voice was silenced with the recent death of Robert E. Wilson, a publisher of several small weeklies in central Illinois. He died on March 16, 1972, of injuries suffered in a car-train accident near Atlanta, Illinois.

Bob Wilson was one of those rare individuals whose entire life was dedicated to working for the welfare of others. As an editor, during his brief excursion into politics, and as a private citizen, he relentlessly championed the causes of the "little people," whether it was an Illinois farmer denied of a fair return for his products; a black southern sharecropper wrongfully disenfranchised; a teen-age soldier in Vietnam forced to fight a war in which he did not believe; or a screaming Vietnamese baby burned by napalm.

He was also a staunch advocate of peace and brotherhood, whose humanitarian and antiwar views were amazingly advanced for their time. In 1962, for example, when the Vietnam War was years away from being a political issue, he was so against the United States' involvement in Southeast Asia that he ran for Congress as a peace candidate, America's Vietnam policy was doomed to failure, he predicted in an editorial that year. He was a man who editorially urged a decade ago that the United States should send its surplus grain to then famine-ravaged Communist China. "It is time the

Reprinted from *Grassroots Editor* 13, no. 4 (July–August 1972): 15–21.

Chinese peasants learn that our system can produce two things that theirs cannot," he wrote, "more food than we can eat, and the compassion to share it with those who have not." And he was a man who in 1967 warned that unless action was taken by the government, America's war economy eventually would drive the nation into a massive depression.

Wilson, who was forty-nine when he died, embarked upon his journalistic career relatively late in life. He was thirty-five when he founded the *Prairie Post* in the tiny farm community of Maroa, Illinois (population, thirteen hundred). Prior to that time, he was a farmer—first, for ten years in Knox County, Missouri and then later in his native Macon County in Illinois. His love for the land and empathy with the small farmer probably were inherited from his paternal ancestors who farmed the corn and soybean land of Macon County through five generations.

"My great-grandfather was a director of the first agricultural society formed in the county, which held our first county fair in 1856," Wilson once said, relating how deeply his farm roots coursed. His grandfather was chairman of the board of county commissioners who organized Macon County and built the log courthouse, still standing in Decatur, where Abraham Lincoln came to practice law.

It was primarily a concern for the plight of the farmer which led Wilson into journalism, according to his Swedish-born wife, Eva. "He was upset with what was happening to the small farmers and over national farm policy," she said. But beyond that, she explained, he could not be entirely satisfied with farming alone. He needed another vehicle for his energy and a means of disseminating his many strong beliefs. When Wilson returned to Illinois after farming in Missouri, he found that Maroa's only newspaper had degenerated to little more than a community bulletin board. After unsuccessfully attempting to buy the owner out, Wilson borrowed two thousand dollars and started his own paper, calling it the *Prairie Post*.

In spite of the small outlay of cash involved, Wilson's plunge into the newspapering business was somewhat adventuresome, and financially risky since he had no prior journalism experience, not even in high school or at Millikin University, from which he graduated in 1943 with a degree in English. However, the winter before he published the first edition of the *Prairie Post,* Wilson did travel around the state visiting weekly editors to learn about the business as best he could.

The first home of the *Prairie Post* was a small corner in the Maroa meat-locker building. There, with the help of his wife, his parents, plus a rented proportional spacing typewriter, a few assorted headline fonts, and a contract with a printer in nearby Decatur who had an offset press, Wilson brought his newspaper into being. That initial edition was rather eye-catching and readable, considering the lack of equipment and experience that went into its production. Nearly half of the front page was filled by a picture of a boyish-looking Wilson pointing to a map of the newspaper's coverage area, above which was a fat headline which proclaimed "A Newspaper Is Born!" The remainder of the front page contained a statement of the newspaper's platform and purpose. "The *Prairie Post* is not a 'shopper' or a 'throwaway,' " the novice editor wrote, "it is a community newspaper." He went on to state that "running a newspaper is a kind of public trust; the motto of the sincere newsman must be: "Ye shall know the truth and the truth shall set you free." Wilson set forth his editorial policy with this warning to foes of the farmer:

"The *Prairie Post* is not tied to any political party, nor to any farm organization. We support those we feel to be acting in the farmer's interests. Those we praise today need not thank us; let them see to it they continue to represent the best interests of the farmers—or tomorrow we may turn around and bite them!" Obviously, Wilson's newspaper was to be farm oriented, but his liberal views on a variety of local, national, and international subjects soon were to emerge in subsequent editions.

From the beginning, Wilson's editorial commentary reflected his belief in peace and equality for all men. As a member of the Society of Friends, Wilson was an avowed pacifist and from young adulthood he put into practice the Quaker teachings of nonviolence and brotherhood. After graduation from college, he worked for nearly two years in a Philadelphia settlement house and in 1944, because of his conscientious objector status, he was drafted into the Civilian Public Service. Instead of wielding a rifle, Wilson fought forest fires in Oregon, worked in a mental hospital in Philadelphia, and

served on a cattleboat which delivered four hundred plow horses
to the farmers of war-devastated Europe.

In 1962, his Quaker beliefs, plus a desire to help the farmer,
led him to seek the office of United States Representative. According to his wife, Wilson ran basically as a peace candidate. In a
booklet of selected editorials which Wilson, who never held public
office, presented as his political "record," he said: "Appalling
though it is to consider, this nation appears to be heading toward
another Korea in South Viet Nam." In his remarkable prophesy
of the impending debacle in Vietnam, Wilson continued:

"Can we have learned so little from the treasure and the blood
we poured into that distant land [Korea]? When will we realize
that the miracles of American industrial production, and the
heroism of American youth, are all wasted if the effort is based
on an insecure political foundation? In Korea we drew a line and
decided all the 'good guys' were on one side, the 'bad guys' on
the other. Actually, almost none of the Koreans on either side
of the line had any idea what Communism was, or what Democracy
was. The situation in South Viet Nam is no better. The Vietnamese
do not know where America is, or why we are there except as
another foreign invader fighting over their soil."

And at the outset of his candidacy, Wilson said: "Our number
one problem is building a world in which peace is possible. I believe
we should challenge the Russians to join us in a step-by-step
advance toward the objective of total disarmament under world
inspection and control."

These were radical positions in an era when peace protests were
seldom in the news and the martial views of groups like the John
Birch Society and the American Legion held sway. Of course,
Wilson anticipated opposition as a result of his liberal opinions
and his conscientious objector status in World War II, but he
probably was not prepared for the vicious smear campaign that
was waged against him. During that campaign, there appeared
on cars and buildings a variety of stickers and posters which were
obviously designed to discredit Wilson's courage and patriotism.
On one such sticker was the international pacifist symbol—the circle
with three converging lines—and the slogan "The Tracks of an
American Chicken." Then on election day, yellow pencils were

distributed at one polling place so, voters were told, they could "properly" mark their ballots for the "coward" Wilson. When the results were finally tabulated, Wilson had captured only 40 percent of the vote, but running on a controversial platform against a strong incumbent, he did much better than anyone had expected. His Kennedyesque charm and physical resemblance to the handsome president helped make Wilson an attractive candidate. But more significantly, the courage of his convictions earned him the respect and votes of thousand of central Illinoisans.

Again in 1971, it was his dedication to world peace that brought him to Paris as a member of a Quaker-sponsored delegation to seek an end to the war in Vietnam. Upon his return, he devoted an entire page in his newspaper to reporting what transpired during the peace mission, frequently interjecting such pithy comments as "We were on the way out [of Vietnam], when Mr. Nixon became inflamed with the lust for military glory and invaded two more countries," and "The [Saigon government's] explanations came out like a broken recording of a Nixon speech."

Throughout his life he courageously defended his convictions, but he was not a man of violence, even when physically threatened. Once an irate candidate for local office struck Wilson in the face over an editorial in which Wilson had questioned the man's competence for public office. Later, nursing a bruised cheek, Wilson told his wife that he did not resist the man's assault because to do so only would have resulted in more violence.

If her husband's anger ever surfaced, Eva Wilson said, it was only in his editorials, which were sometimes vitriolic, but never hateful. Every edition, he composed two or three lengthy, cogent editorials, usually writing them on weekends at his farm home outside Maroa. Although his newspaper did an adequate job of reporting the local news, it was these editorials that distinguished the *Prairie Post* and its editor. Wilson's commentary generally was localized, but he often expressed his views on the Washington scene and world affairs as well. "He ran a small country newspaper," a Decatur newsman wrote shortly after Wilson's death, "but he managed to think country without thinking small."

Big business, big government, and big agriculture were the targets at which Wilson most frequently leveled his editorial guns. However, he also took time to comment on more mundane topics. In one issue, for example, he warned readers to be wary of bogus termite inspectors who were operating in the Maroa area; called for cheaper construction of swimming pools so that even small towns like his own could afford to give their residents "a sky blue pool of cool water to plunge into on these August days"; and commended Macon County Fair officials for removing from a "house of horrors" on the fairgrounds a mock gravestone and a sign which read, "Earl Warren: Expect Him Soon."

Wilson's most intense editorial efforts were on behalf of the farmer and the small-town way of life which he so strongly felt should be preserved. It distressed him to see the small farmer denied, and sometimes cheated, of a fair return for his labors. Wilson himself had difficulty making ends meet as a farmer, thus he knew the problems of earning a living from the soil and editorially fought for fair treatment of the farmer. In one instance, the *Prairie Post* revealed how agriculture leaders had announced a soybean surplus which meant farmers would receive a much lower price for their products when they brought them to soybean processing plants. The National Farmers Organization, suspecting price-fixing, formed a massive "buying action" to determine if the surplus actually existed. But when hundreds of Midwest farmers descended upon Decatur, the "soybean capital of the world," they discovered that there were only two hundred tons of soybean meal in the entire city, far less than could be considered a surplus. Just who was responsible for the false report of a surplus was not clear, but Editor Wilson stated:

"The strong probability is that a deception has taken place and that it is now sufficiently exposed so that the Justice Department can examine the situation with an eye to prosecution under the anti-trust laws for conspiring to fix prices. When the back of this conspiracy has been broken, farmers may be able to go into the marketplace as equals and sell for $2.75, $3.00, or some price that will return them the cost of production plus a reasonable profit."

Wilson's most bitter editorials were directed at the national leadership of the Farm Bureau, an organization which he believes to be "antifarmer," and whose "interests, policies, and activities are identical with those of the big business community." His alle-

giance was pledged to the National Farmers Organization, which
Wilson considered a true friend of the farmer. "The NFO," he
once wrote, "like the Farmers Union and the Grange, is run by
the farmers and works for their interests." Other agricultural organizations, he said, "did nothing for the farmer but collect dues."

This abiding concern for the farmer's welfare prompted Wilson's
most determined and successful editorial campaign. At issue was
a referendum on a junior college for the Decatur area. Wilson
was opposed not to the establishment of the junior college, but
to the unfair property tax assessment with which the junior college
was to be financed. Under Illinois law, as Wilson repeatedly pointed
out in news stories and editorials, industrial property was assessed
at 27½ percent, while farm land was assessed at 55 percent. "Farmers, with one-third the income," he editorially urged, "are expected
to pay three times as much as Decatur industry. In relation to
income, rural people are going to pay six times as much as big
industry, the people who will profit most from a junior college."

In a sample copy of the *Prairie Post* which was sent to every
rural household in the proposed college district the day before
the referendum, Wilson said:

"We are not 'against education' any more than you are, but we
are against any more tax increases under the present unfair and
outdated tax on real estate, which penalizes the farmers. . . .
No, we cannot afford to print and mail so many thousand papers.
We work for what money we have. But neither can we afford to
let this thing go without a fight."

Also in that same sample copy was an editorial cartoon by Wilson
which depicted a farmer pinched between the twin arms of a
grappler labeled "high taxes" and "low prices." Not content to
fight with just his typewriter, Wilson carried his campaign outside
the pages of his newspaper to form and lead a group called Action
Committee For Fair Taxes, which issued pamphlets and held
forums in opposition to the referendum. The combined effort of
Wilson and the Action Committee had its intended effect, because
the referendum was soundly defeated not only once, but again
in a second round of balloting a year later.

The energy Wilson expended in his junior college campaign
apparently came from a limitless reservoir that drove him like a

human dynamo from early morning, when he daily jogged a mile around his home in Argenta, Illinois, to late evenings, when he would spend hours either writing stories or planning the format of another edition of the *Prairie Post*. His normal work schedule would have exhausted the average man. Early morning hours were spent at farm chores, although a whiplash injury in an auto accident ultimately reduced much of his farming activities. On Mondays and Tuesdays, his afternoons were spent soliciting ads and collecting news items. He received assistance from his father with advertising sales, and his wife and mother did typing and office work. But Wilson, with the exception of news briefs contributed by correspondents in neighboring communities, wrote and edited all the copy, laid out and pasted up every page, composed every headline, drew cartoons, and even took some pictures.

Wednesdays were primarily devoted to getting the paper ready for press. According to Eva Wilson, her husband was extremely particular about the appearance of his newspaper, often spending hours attempting to achieve a perfectly balanced front-page layout. Of course, the balanced effect, once a popular layout format, did not make for as streamlined and attractive a page as more modern typography might have made, but Wilson took pride in his efforts. The inside pages often were solid blocks of copy broken only by an assortment of local ads, many of which were designed by Wilson. The pictures and artwork which were used frequently were so large that they dominated the page at the expense of the news.

The *Prairie Post*, however, did become more attractive as Wilson gained in experience and acquired better equipment. In its early days, for instance, the newspaper was without a headliner machine. As a result, small heads were set on a typewriter equipped with special block lettering. Larger heads had to be hand set with adhesive-backed paper fonts. Later, Wilson purchased a headliner, and then a Fairchild web offset press, proudly displaying a large picture of the new piece of machinery on the front page of the *Prairie Post*. While the appearance of Wilson's newspaper improved, so did the editorial writing of its editor. "His first editorials were not as good as his later one," Eva Wilson apologetically explained. She pointed out that her husband was not a novice writer when he began the *Prairie Post*, having written in 1952 the

novel *Aideen MacLennon,* the story of a young conscientious objector. But initially he did not have the experience at the persuasive,
concise language of the newspaper editorial, she said. Thus his
early editorial efforts were sometimes rambling, literary essays.
However, in time, he developed an effective, multifaceted style
of his own.

Wilson's editorial voice often changed to meet his mood or subject
matter. He could be quaintly homespun in one instance and sophisticated in another. Or he could be caustic, then eloquent. Occasionally, his editorials were exercises in verbal rage. "Don't go
to Alabama," he angrily wrote after a jury there acquitted a Ku
Klux Klan member of a murder charge. "If some smartaleck loafer
from the village square does not like your face . . . he may stick
a revolver in your car window and blow your head off." At other
times his editorials were expressions of his dry sense of humor.
After being defeated in the 1962 congressional race, Wilson left
the entire editorial column of the *Prairie Post* blank, commenting
to his wife that "there is just nothing more to say." A favorite
device of Wilson's was satire, which he used bitterly following John
F. Kennedy's assassination. He wrote:

"We regret the criticism of Dallas police authorities by national
press representatives; we are confident they gave Kennedy, and
later Oswald, all the police protection they thought necessary. . . .
We salute the Great State of Texas and its spirit of self-reliant
independence. It will always be famous as the home of gun-toting
men of action who solve their own problems without waiting on
others to do it for them."

It was the cause of peace, however, which brought out Wilson's
finest writing and his most provocative commentary. In 1964, long
before any liberal members of the metropolitan press had spoken
out, Wilson deplored the use of napalm in Vietnam which, he wrote,
"indiscriminately killed schoolboys, suckling babes and grandmas,
as well as men of fighting age who may—or may not—take part
in nighttime Viet Cong raids." Calling Vietnam "McNamara's
War," Wilson urged the then secretary of defense to view the
destruction and death American bombs were causing. "Has he
visited a native village after our bombs struck it, and looked into
the burned faces of dead children who never heard of either Communism or Democracy?" he rhetorically asked in a plaintive edito-

rial. A year later a powerful Wilson editorial cried out against the government subsidies paid to aluminum, steel, and copper producers. According to the outspoken editor:

"Sixteen millions for cancer research was called 'socialism,' and your Congressmen voted against it. . . . Billions for subsidies to the metal industries must be something else, because [the Congressmen] voted for that every time. One of the major pressures for war in this country comes from manufacturers who can sell more products . . . if steel tanks rust in the rice paddies and aluminum helicopters crash in the jungles. If our boys die in the mud of a colonial war halfway around the world, remember the aluminum in the dogtags around their necks."

Then early in 1970, before the American program to bequeath the war effort to the Army of the Republic of Vietnam was labeled a failure by many press observers, Wilson commented: "Vietnamization is a face-saving device employed to let us get out of an impossible situation. It is so fragile a falsehood that every one involved is tiptoeing around lest it should shatter."

Wilson also sharpened his editorial teeth on the "establishment press." In the tradition of a colleague for whom he had great respect, the late Eugene Cervi, publisher of *Cervi's Rocky Mountain Journal*, Wilson denounced the monopolistic practices of the media giants which he felt were driving many independent publishers out of business. Wilson often used the occasion of Newspaper Week to launch a diatribe against the mass-media industry. "Our naturally non-conformist tendencies causes us, nearly every year, to even the score by roasting our own profession, just as warmly as we do any other," he explained in one editorial. Another time he suggested to his readers "not to believe half of what newspapers tell you about themselves. Many newspapermen believe that newspapers are written for idiots: many of their readers assume they are written by idiots. It is difficult to say where the truth lies." In a more serious vein, he commented on an alarming form of indirect press censorship in Vietnam. "War correspondents," he wrote, "are now accompanied by Information Officers who encourage them to take a 'more positive' viewpoint. So we have the spate of articles quoting soldiers who say they believe in what they are doing."

Frequently, Wilson's indignation would boil over the boundaries of his editorial columns and seep into the *Prairie Post*'s news pages. In his campaign against the junior college referendum, for example, one front-page headline pointly declared: "Bleed Agriculture to Build Industry." A "kicker" above the main head read "The Master Plan for Higher Education in Illinois," with the word "Education" struck out by a bold red "X" and in its place substituted the word "Taxes." The "story" beneath the headlines was actually a lengthy editorial outlining how farmers traditionally have been burdened by unfair taxation. In addition, Wilson would sometimes take news service photographs and with his own captions, covert them into not too subtle editorial vignettes. Once he ran a picture of a clean-shaven twenty-two-year-old student who was arrested after burning his draft card. "Does he look like a criminal to you?" Wilson asked in reference to a new federal law which made it a crime punishable by a five-year jail sentence for failure to possess a draft card. In fact, some issues of the *Prairie Post* were so permeated with Wilson's opinion, the entire newspaper had the appearance of an immense editorial.

While Wilson can be criticized for allowing his views to distort his objectivity, he can be praised for steadfastly refusing to compromise his convictions. He belonged to that small fraternity of publishers who put principles before profits, as he demonstrated in the first issue of the *Prairie Post*. Stating his newspaper's policy, he said: "We will not print any advertising we feel to be false, misleading, or harmful." In a following issue he elaborated on that policy, explaining why his paper would not carry the ads of cigarette or liquor manufacturers. "Such advertisements are very profitable to a newspaper," he wrote, "and it is no trick to get them; but if this editor is forced to sell lung cancer and cirrhosis of the liver in order to make a profit, he will do without the profit."

Wilson's sharp criticism of the Illinois Power & Light Company also cost him advertising dollars. "Each time IPL would place an ad in the paper, Robert would invariably carry a story attacking the company's electrical service, and future ads would be canceled," Eva Wilson said.

When a severe snow and ice storm caused heavy damage to IPL power lines leading into Maroa, Wilson devoted an entire front page to "stories" in which he concurrently condemned the IPL and praised the local consumer-owned electrical cooperative, which he felt had the interest of the rural population at heart. Beneath a picture showing power lines snapped under the weight of a heavy coating of ice, Wilson remarked: "A city of 1300 people deserves heavy transmission cables that do not pop like dry spaghetti under an ice load." Elsewhere on the page, after documenting his case against Illinois Power & Light, he somewhat boastfully asked: "Have you read these facts anywhere else? What other newspaper would dare to tell it the way it is?"

With nearly every issue, Wilson's controversial positions would result in canceled subscriptions and advertising. During the junior college battle, in particular, many regular advertisers in Decatur dropped their advertisements apparently in opposition to the editor's stand. Then, too, his attacks on the John Birch Society, whose methods he once termed as "Hitlerism in America," resulted in reprisals by local Birchers designed to encourage subscribers and advertisers to desert the liberal publisher. The *Prairie Post*'s profit sheet was also hurt by Wilson's commentary on the Vietnam War and in one instance prompted a window-breaking foray on his office. After the incident Wilson ran a picture of himself pointing to the broken window with the caption: "Peace is worth the price, even if fanatics scream at us on the radio talk shows, and both of our plate glass windows are broken hours after we go on TV asking a withdrawal from Vietnam. Are you prepared to pay the price of peace?

Once, with a smile on his face, Wilson told his family that he could afford to buy a new car each year with the revenue from the advertisement he either refused to accept or those which he drove away with his outspokenness.

Wilson, though, was not entirely insensitive to the pressures felt by many small-town editors. When the *Prairie Post* failed to report the results of a local softball tournament, Wilson sheepishly apologized with an editorial entitled "We Missed the Ball." In an attempt to explain the oversight, he said, "A few may suppose we ignored the tournament because it was sponsored by a tavern. That is rubbish." But Wilson did not allow local pressures to temper his liberal commentary, which alternately shocked, amused, informed, stimulated, and angered his readers. Eva Wilson recalled how

Maroa residents would stand outside of the post office on Thursday mornings eagerly awaiting the latest edition of the *Prairie Post* to see who was going to be the next victim of Bob Wilson's editorial wrath. Enough readers and advertisers supported Wilson to enable him to expand his publications to include six other weeklies. With profits from his modest strings of newspapers, he founded and published the *Illinois Farmer,* which had as its slogan, "A Magazine for the Farmer Who Thinks for Himself." Immediately, the *Illinois Farmer* became another vehicle for Wilson's philosophy and an organ for the National Farmer's Organization. The magazine also afforded Wilson the opportunity to present his own views on complex farm and economic issues. In one article which demonstrated the depth and breadth of his knowledge of the United States monetary system, Wilson wrote:

"Federal income tax deducted from wage checks does not go at once to the government. First it is deposited in banks all over the country where it lies without interest until the government decides to call for it. Last year an average of 5.3 billion dollars in such funds lay on deposit in banks. At 4 percent interest, this lost the taxpayers 212 million dollars in twelve months time. What do they (the banks) do with these funds? They either lend them to you, or buy U.S. bonds. When they buy bonds, they collect interest from the government on the government's own money!

Just prior to his death, Bob Wilson showed signs that he was planning to reduce the grueling pace at which he drove himself. He had sold several of his smaller papers and had decided to retain only the twenty-five-hundred-circulation *Prairie Post,* the largest of his publications. "He just realized he was spreading himself too thin," Eva Wilson said. Ironically, he was killed while returning from Atlanta, Illinois, after discussing the sale of his newspaper there with a prospective buyer. After his death, Robert E. Wilson's body was cremated and his ashes were carried by the wind across the farmland he so dearly loved and defended. His loss was felt keenly by his family, friends, and loyal readers. But everyone concerned with the preservation of his brand of independent, courageous journalism should likewise lament at Robert E. Wilson's passing.

Pedro Calomarde
Underground Editor

Mason Rossiter Smith

The story had its beginnings in July, 1942, in the Philippines' darkest days of World War II, and it wasn't concluded until March, 1945. In those first cataclysmic days, the Japanese—having forced the surrender of the American and Filipino forces on Corregidor, taken over the city of Manila, and gradually overrun most of the Philippine Commonwealth—began methodically to seek out and kill elements of the resistance movement.

But a tough-bitted newspaperman of Cebu (he's a disarmingly pleasant, charming chap when you meet him now, in peacetime), a printer-publisher by the name of Cipriano A. Barba, later to be brevetted a captain in the Philippine forces, was determined that the morale of his people must be maintained. Assigned to the publicity section of the resistance movement. Barba—from a secret hideout in the mountain above Cebu City—directed publication of two underground papers, *Torch* and *Kadaugan,* copies of which not only were distributed with reasonable regularity to the Filipino fighting forces but were actually smuggled under the very noses of Japanese patrols, sentries, and secret agents into the Japanese-controlled areas of the archipelago, even into the city of Cebu.

As copies of the clandestine newspapers came to hand, the Nipponese high command at once attempted to trace the source, and in an effort to wipe out this vital communications link in the resistance movement, sent troops into the mountains to hunt the printers down. But Captain Barba and his men were not this easily dismayed: they merely dug cavities in the soft earth of the mountainsides and buried their equipment.

"That," he observed some years later, when Pedro Calomarde introduced us at the "just a little lunch" session one morning in Cebu, "isn't the conventional treatment for type and a printing press, but in times like these one does what one must."

The Japanese went back chagrined and empty-handed. Once

Reprinted from *Grassroots Editor* 1, no. 2 (April 1960): 3–4, 29.

they had trooped back into Cebu City, Captain Barba engaged the services of Pedro Calomarde as editor and started up all over again—this time with a number of refinements. The new paper was called *Morning Times,* and it appeared regularly on Saturdays.

It was still a small newspaper, in size, though large in influence. Made up in four and sometimes six pages, two columns wide, page size 5½ by 8½ inches, it was printed on newsprint, one page at a time (and often one column or even part of one column at a time), occasionally in two and three colors, as before, on an old 9-by-12 hand-fed, foot-pedal-operated Chandler & Price press. This type of machine is known in the Philippines as a "Minerva," the name having stuck in much the same way that many an American calls any make of electric refrigerator a Frigidaire or a Kelvinator.

Type was set entirely by hand, and when there wasn't enough type to set up a full column or a full page, the publishers simply printed whatever amount of copy their type supply would permit, tore the form down, distributed the type, and started the process all over again, repeating it and repeating it until all four pages were complete.

The "refinements" however, included an old prewar Royal portable typewriter, which Pedro showed me in his office years later, still in operation despite its scars of war. When I saw it, the fabric of the top cover loosened by moisture in the jungle, had been crudely pasted back on its boards and frayed corners betrayed rough usage. The machine itself was oiled, in surprisingly good operating condition, and the ribbon was black.

"Yes," Pedro smiled, "it still works pretty good. Back in those days, of course, it was pretty hard to come by a typewriter ribbon so we had to make the one we had last as long as possible—by rubbing coconut oil on it." The typewriter, he added, had undergone just about every possible kind of experience short of destruction itself. "It was a pretty vital piece of equipment," he recalled, "and I'll never forget how once we almost lost it."

In the tropics, the jungle often grows so thick that a man crashing through it cannot hear another only a few yards away. Thus it was that when the Japs almost surprised the editor in his cave one morning, Pedro had just time enough to push the typewriter up onto a rocky ledge above his head, scrape some leaves over it, and melt into the jungle greenery just ahead of the intruders. "They didn't find it," he grinned, "but I didn't dare go back there for a long time, either. When I did, the typewriter was all right, only a bit rusty."

In addition to the typewriter, Captain Barba and his forces had managed also to conjure up a radio receiving set and eventually even a hydroelectric power plant—with the result that the *Morning Times,* printed inside a cave up in the mountains of Cangondo Barili on the western shore of the island of Cebu, was able to boast surprisingly full and up-to-date coverage not only of the war in the Pacific but in Europe as well. Leading newscasters and news commentators were unwitting contributors to a newspaper which did much to keep up the morale of the fighting forces and the people of the Philippines.

Indeed, one of Pedro Calomarde's proudest memories is that of distributing General MacArthur's Christmas message in 1944. Forwarded to the jungle printing plant by resistance headquarters in Cebu, the message was printed in leaflet form and distributed throughout the province—again, even in the city of Cebu which was then under the theoretically tight control of the Japanese.

The *Morning Times* frankly and fearlessly discussed the military and naval campaigns, the shifting and replacement of high Japanese officers, even conditions in the Nipponese homeland itself—all of which had been withheld by the military from Japanese soldiers in the Philippines.

"The battle for Ormoc," Calomarde wrote in the edition of November 18, 1944, "is the battle for the Philippines, and the battle for the Philippines is the battle for China, Burma and India. . . . The Liberty-loving people are awaiting the result. Even Tokyo is concentrating its attention on the Philippine war front. This is shown by the general shakeup of the Japanese high command. . . . The loyal Filipinos are in the front line."

The editor continued to pound home this victory theme, taunting the Japanese to surrender and sue for peace before it was too late. Above the front-page masthead on Saturday, March 17, 1945, Editor Calomarde ran this headline in red ink: "300 Giant Bombers

Hit Japanese Cities," and just under it, "Yanks Land in Zamboanga and Rombion." This week he began to make use of the newspaper's "ears" for war-winning slogans.

They changed weekly, reading; "Don't hoard food; Help our soldiers"; "Farm work is war work; Carry on with corn, camotes"; "Americans bring light; Freedom is dawning"; "Help build Cebu City; Cooperate with Gov't"; "You helped win the war; Now help win the peace."

Eventually, *Morning Times* was to taste its greatest triumph when it could publish a six-page edition (vol. 2, no. 16), Saturday March 31, 1945—the front page printed in red, blue and black ink, with the red banner headline: "Solomons Veterans Liberate Cebu City." Beneath it was another equally as big in black: "Japanese Retreat As Americans Advance."

A photograph of President Roosevelt printed blue, carried these cutlines beneath: "At all times the Filipino people will always look upon President Franklin D. Roosevelt of the United States as their great liberator and benefactor. To him they are ever grateful for making the Philippines a pattern of civilization in the Orient."

Week by week, *Morning Times* recorded the growing, often sad and bitter story of victory—"U.S. Army, Marine Forces Invade Okinawa"; "F. D. Roosevelt dies at 63 Years of Age"; "Allied Armies Begin Battle for Berlin"—until finally Editor Calomarde could report the capitulation of the German forces in Europe and the signing of the Japanese surrender document in Tokyo.

But until vol. 2, no. 20, the dateline under the front page masthead carried no indication of where *Morning Times* was printed—there was only the laconic statement under the nameplate itself: "Published by instructions of the High Command, 82nd Division, PA [Philippine Army]." In this issue for the first time, the dateline read: "Cebu City, Saturday 28 April 1945." The banner headline just below it said: "U.S. Filipino Forces Pursue Japs in Cebu"—the reason, perhaps, why it wasn't yet safe to put names in the editorial page masthead—for, with thousands of Japanese yet to be flushed out of their foxholes in the jungles, the war was still far from finished in the Philippines.

In its edition for May 10, 1945, *Morning Times* came out on Thursday—and for the first time since the paper was published the editorial masthead read like this:

Morning Times
Published Thursday & Saturday
Capt. Cipriano A. Barba
Publications Officer
Pedro D. Calomarde
Editor

Now the newspaper began to dedicate its efforts to winning the peace. "The return of democracy to the Philippines," the editor wrote in that edition, "revives the people's will which is always voiced in the press. Without a free press the people's will is dead and democracy becomes a farce."

Week after week, Calomarde discussed the developing victory and the need for loyalty and harmony at home. "The people's confidence in their government depends upon the men that run the machinery of the government. . . . The newly established Philippine government demands loyal public servants. When collaborationists of the Japanese administration enter in the government sphere of influence by holding public office, the people's confidence in the government is wanting."

Again, "The indigents in the city of Cebu constitute a social problem of the first degree . . . a direct challenge to the government and to the social workers. . . . The progress of any community is gauged by the social condition of the people living in it." And, "The masses of the people . . . rescued from three years of Jap domination urgently need rehabilitation of their moral and spiritual life. A moral crusade should be launched [against] looting and petty thievery. . . . A campaign must be directed toward the elimination of all Japanese evil influences." This was during the difficult postwar days of the corrupt Quirino regime, and before the appearance of the late, beloved President Ramon Magsaysay on the political scene.

America had kept her promise; the Philippines had become an independent nation, but the war here as all over the world, had left its mark. As in the early days of the new republic of the United States, corrupt politics produced disrespect for law, and political decisions were often settled in the provinces with a gun. The life of a crusading editor often was in danger, as a result.

But Pedro Calomarde survived, the paper eventually changed from a biweekly to a Friday publication, and in time grew into

the full-sized tabloid it is today, published Tuesday, Thursday and
Sunday. Meanwhile, Editor Calomarde acquired the newspaper
from Captain Barba, who retains his commercial printing firm—it
still prints the *Morning Times* for its present owner. And determined, patriotic Filipino that he is, Pedro Calomarde continues
to fight for a better Cebu, a better Philippines. "As long as I live,"
he told me seriously, "there will always be a *Morning Times.* It
is my life."

The People of Clinton
Were with Us

Horace V. Wells, Jr.

When the opposition to integration of Clinton High School developed it was entirely unexpected. The actual process of integration
had begun many months before the start of school. In fact the
federal court order setting the date of integration was handed down
in late December, 1955, and it was not to be effective until the
start of the next school term, in August, 1956.

When the storm broke, I did not canvass the community to find
out how my advertisers and my subscribers stood on the matter.
My reaction to the violence was the same as that to be expected
of any other editor who might have stood in my shoes. "We must
have law and order. We must obey constituted authority. We cannot
have the alternative, which would be anarchy."

Fortunately an overwhelming majority of the people in my area
felt the same way. This does not mean they issued statements,
or even came forward publicly and took a stand. In fact most of
them were careful not to take a public stand, one merchant even
going so far as to refuse to sign a community-sponsored telegram
asking the governor to send the National Guard to protect the
town from the mobs!

How did I know they felt the same way I did? When you have
lived with people for twenty-five years—I was born in South Caro-

Reprinted from *Grassroots Editor* 1, no. 2 (April 1960): 11–12, 24.

lina, lived in Nashville, Tennessee, from 1919 to 1933 and was graduated from Vanderbilt University, moving to Clinton in 1933 to start my newspaper—you know them pretty well. This is especially true of a small town, and Clinton is still a town of under five thousand population.

I knew how Mayor W. E. Lewallen felt, for he and his board of mayor and aldermen took every step they could to see that laws were obeyed and that order was maintained. When the situation got beyond the town's ability to handle it—with mobs of outsiders pouring in to cause the trouble—they unanimously requested Governor Frank Clement to send the National Guard.

I knew how the president of the high school PTA felt about it—for Mrs. Harry F. Miller issued a statement from her executive board when children stayed out of school, begging their parents to send them back in order that their education might not be impaired.

I knew how my advertisers felt about it, for after my editorial stand had been made clear, only one or two of them refused to continue their normal advertising practices. In our Christmas issue, in which practically every firm in the area normally inserts greetings, only two or three refused to take an advertisement on the grounds they did not approve of our stand in the integration troubles.

I knew how the board of education stood, for I saw them refuse to knuckle under to demands of the newly organized and highly vociferous White Citizens Council and assert their position as obeying the orders of the courts.

I knew how the students of Clinton High School felt, for my youngest daughter was a freshman there and because I knew they voted unanimously by secret ballot to stand behind their principal, D. J. Brittain, Jr., who was one of the targets of those opposed to integration and whose life was made miserable by threats upon him and upon his wife who also was a member of the school staff.

And I also knew how many of my subscribers felt, for after I had taken my stand many came in and told me they were behind me.

I knew how the churches stood, for when the Reverend Paul Turner, pastor of Clinton First Baptist Church issued an invitation for men to walk with him as he escorted the Negro children to school between lines of threatening and jeering white men and women, the chairman of his deacon board, Attorney Sidney Davis, and a steward of the Methodist church, Leo Burnett, walked with him.

But, in the community were many whose hatreds, whose passions had been aroused. Before the troublemaker, John Frederick Kasper, came to town and stirred the people up, these hatreds were buried deep within the people and little was said. They didn't like having the Negro children admitted to the school, but they didn't say anything. Kasper in his stirring speeches caused these hatreds to flame and the passions to overflow. Before Kasper came, the white and Negro children had attended school together one day without incident—they all had known for eight months it was to be that way. After Kasper came, then also came the riots and later the dynamitings, and two years later the blasting of the school.

After the first troubles had quieted and the National Guard had gone, things were peaceful for a while because most of the people respected the federal court order prohibiting interference with the integration order. This order was handed down while Kasper was causing trouble, and when he violated it, he found himself sentenced to six months in the federal prison.

But Kasper remained out on bond, appealing his case to the U.S. Supreme Court. During this period, about two months after the initial troubles, an undercover campaign of intimidation was begun, against the Negro students who were attending school, against the school principal, against the mayor of Clinton, and against the newspaper editor.

The campaign was also extended to include anyone who refused to contribute to the White Citizens Council or to any politician who refused to go along with their requests. "nigger lover" became an effective weapon as well as a hated epithet, and it was used effectively as a means of intimidation.

In the spring of 1957 there was a series of so-far unexplained and unsolved dynamite blasts at various places over the community. One of the blasts was in the front yard of Chief of Police Francis Moore, who also was a member of the school board. Another was in my front yard. Others were in the Negro section. Fortunately the only damages were shattered nerves, a few broken windows and many hours of lost sleep!

About this time a new weekly newspaper was started. The new newspaper was openly dedicated to the cause of segregation and to the elimination of the *Clinton Courier-News.* In an article written for the *Charleston* (S.C.) *News and Courier,* that newspaper's staff reporter predicted the end of the *Courier-News,* with the new *Tennessee Reporter,* which said it was "printing the news people want to read," as the successor.

Although during the troubles of the fall and early winter of 1956 the circulation of the *Courier-News* reached four thousand, the advent of the new newspaper and a door-to-door and house-to-house campaign by the White Citizens Council and segregationists sponsoring it, caused it to drop with a crash to the three thousand mark in the Audit Bureau of Circulation's report for the first quarter of 1957.

Although our newspaper gained several new customers for its printing department from nearby Oak Ridge during this period, advertising was off. Threats of boycott affected some of the merchants, while the general unrest in the community (any kind of unrest hurts business) probably was the direct cause of the drop, although the business recession of 1957 is bound to have had some effect. After the first quarter of 1957, although the *Tennessee Reporter* held on until July—losing money all the time—our circulation started back up and now we are at new heights—our press run being 4,350 and our ABC figure is back to the 4,000 mark.

Negro children have continued to attend Clinton High School, and at no time did the responsible people of the community or the school authorities consider closing the schools to prevent them from attending. One Negro boy was graduated in the class of 1957, but there were no Negro seniors in 1958. Only about a half a dozen Negros are included in the nine-hundred student enrollment.

The situation was the same, in spite of the fact that the school on October 5, 1958, was destroyed by three huge dynamite blasts set off in different sections of the building. Since then, the children (Negroes and white) have been using temporary facilities and an empty elementary school building in Oak Ridge. And there have been many prayers that the new school (which will be ready in the fall of 1960) will not suffer a similar fate.

Whether or not the community supported our position would

have made no difference in our attitude on this issue. At the same time I wonder and have wondered many times how effective we might have been if the community had not agreed. I have wondered also how long the *Courier-News* would have remained in business.

The facts are that the finances of our newspaper—which we started from scratch in 1939—are such that we could not long have withstood the loss of any sizeable amount of revenue and continued to operate. Then, too our circulation distribution system was extremely vulnerable as two-thirds of our papers are sold by newsboys and dealers with only one-third handled through the mail on a paid-in-advance basis.

Had our community disagreed with us and wanted no more of us, all it needed to do was stop advertising and stop buying copies of the paper! How long could we have operated without advertising or circulation? Fortunately efforts to bring this about failed and we are still here.

But, as we write this our thoughts turn to the wonderfully brave Mabel Norris Reese at Mt. Dora, Florida, and to courageous John F. Wells of Little Rock, Arkansas. They can testify to the value of having a community behind you and they will tell you how fortunate we have been here in Clinton to have such support. It takes courage to be different, but it takes infinitely more courage to be different if your very existence is threatened and if you must stand alone. We can lay claim to neither of these to any great degree.

We have often thought of Elijah Parish Lovejoy. He is praised and honored by newspapermen today for his heroic stand for the principles in which he believed. But what did it get him, we ask ourselves. His printing presses were destroyed, his newspaper was ended, and his life was taken.

Today newspaper editors who stand up for the things in which they believe often must face possible economic loss for their newspapers, and some of them are in areas where certain stands would likely bring the destruction of their plants from dynamiting or the loss of their homes through arson.

Standing alone, daring to be different bring great satisfaction for a while; the awards that sometimes accompany such stands are beautiful, and the amount of public recognition is wonderful, but none of these pay salaries, paper bills or buy Linotype metal. And none of them make up for the hours of lost sleep. It also is true that most of us are cowards. We work for economic security and we don't throw it away easily. Therefore, if we deliberately consider some of the courses we find ourselves taking, our courage may fail us.

As for myself, I did not deliberately choose the editorial path I was to follow. I really had no other choice. I merely said what I have always believed and I said it without consideration of the consequences. Now, as we look back, we give thanks for the fact that our community—generally speaking—was behind us all the time.

How to Be a Man
of Distinction
P. D. East

My claim to distinction, actually is twofold. First, I own a weekly newspaper in the village of Petal, located two miles from the town of Hattiesburg, in Forrest County, Mississippi, and my newspaper has the lowest local per capita circulation of any in the world. I confess to an abounding ignorance of arithmetic, but I think in dealing with material objects the lowest count is zero. And zero is the number which represents my circulation in Petal (whose own claim to distinction is, as proud Petalites will tell you, that it is "the largest unincorporated town in the country").

Second, my paper is, to the best of my knowledge, the only one in the nation with an unlisted telephone number. I wish to point out that to reduce a local circulation from twenty-three hundred to zero in only five years requires a certain ability and constant effort. I say that with pride, of course. Frankly, you've got to work at it full time—and a ringing telephone is distracting.

My distinction makes certain demands, and to date the price I've paid has been two ulcers, a pointed head of gray hair, and

Reprinted from *Grassroots Editor* 2, no. 2 (April 1961): 11, 29–30.

almost fifteen thousand dollars in cash. I'll admit my success was not a sure thing in the beginning. Actually, the first hint of it came when a mop-maker refused his paper at the post office one week. It was returned to me marked "refused," and I was surprised, but in the weeks which followed I became accustomed to an armful every Friday. And with those refused papers I knew I'd arrived.

The secret of my first sweet smell of success was relatively simple. I had reached a startling conclusion: that Negroes were, after all, just people. Needless to say, I was more than a little surprised to learn that everyone didn't share my opinion. I reached this conclusion from reading the Constitution of the United States, and especially the amendments to it, which impressed me and wouldn't turn loose from my memory. Having been so corrupted, I was shocked at a proposed amendment to the constitution of the state of Mississippi, put to a vote in the fall of 1954, which empowered the state legislature to abolish the public school system in the event of integration.

My best advertiser—who, by his own modest admission, was the leading merchant in the village—told me that anyone who opposed the amendment was for the integration of white schools. He was an articulate man and got the message across: if I opposed the amendment he would stop advertising. I opposed it, true to my conscience; he stopped advertising, true to his word. We were both honorable men. I stopped to reflect and concluded that success didn't "just happen." I saw right away I'd have to work at it, which I did. In a short time I didn't have a single advertiser in Petal.

Having been corrupted by the Constitution, I decided it was my patriotic duty to render a service to my state. I did so in presenting an editorial, on April 21, 1955, suggesting that the state symbol of the Magnolia be replaced with the crawfish: "Here in the State of Mississippi we are making progress, progress such as no state heretofore has known. Our sagacious leaders are showing us how; they are leading the way. Their aim is to protect us from those crawfish who haven't the intelligence to move backward (as any sane crawfish knows), backward toward the mud from which he came."

The reaction was of some interest, especially the fact that something like five professional southerners bought subscriptions to the paper, telling me how pleased they were that I'd made it clear to "them niggers as to their place." I was proud to take their money.

In the meantime, I decided to support a friend of long standing in his race for the office of county sheriff. He had asked me to support him, and I knew of no reason why I shouldn't. During the campaign I had occasion to call on him at his home twice. Both times I found myself cooling my heels on the front lawn. Not once was I invited in. Being a sensitive soul, I began to wonder about my social standing in the community.

Admittedly, it took a little time for the situation to dawn on me, but now I know—there are four homes in the entire county to which I can go and not have to sit on the lawn. And to those four, I confess, I'm never invited. In any event I have a plan. Should my dear friend decide to seek the sheriff's office in the next election he will have my full support—whether he wants it or not.

That same year I opposed a gentleman seeking reelection to his office. My opposition was based on the fact that he had stood on his hind legs in the courthouse of Forrest County at a meeting of school board members and said that whites and "coloreds" could not meet together. The dozen or so Negro citizens present had been invited to the meeting by the school board members, all of which were white. In short, the gentleman played to the gallery (and the press) and in five minutes did harm to the race relations that couldn't be repaired in five years.

My personal impression was not a favorable one, and having run out of ideas for editorial copy on the blessings and wonders of American Motherhood, I felt inclined to comment on that act by a real, 100 percent, red-blooded professional southerner. While I've never claimed that the gentleman was responsible for it, I will point out that for two days and one night thereafter my wife was shadowed by an unknown person. I think it was a war of nerves, and I think whoever was responsible came close to winning, because my wife got quite nervous, believe me.

Shortly after my comments on the behavior of the professional southerner, I happened into the post office in Hattiesburg and a lady stopped me and said: "Are you P. D. East?" Thinking she just might want to spend five dollars for a subscription to my paper, I admitted that I was. (I have since learned to keep my mouth shut in such circumstances, except to say: "No, I'm sorry, I'm God, but I've got my eye on that fellow.") She fixed me with a steady gaze and said: "I'm of half a mind to wring your neck."

Still in pursuit of success, I took a stand in a telephone strike. My position was that labor had every right to bargain, to negotiate, and to strike, should its members decide; but it did not have the right to destroy property, public or private, nor did the members have the right to beat up employees who did not belong to the union.

I fear my simple position was misunderstood by all concerned. On a Saturday night, following the statement of my position, my home telephone began to ring. Eight times it tolled, and each time for me, and each time it represented a canceled subscription, coupled with a verbal blow. Finally, I left the telephone off the hook.

It was during the strike that I received my first threat of a beating. The unidentified gentleman was nice about it: he was just going to knock my brains out—nothing really serious. Anyway, it would have been quite a feat, considering that other callers had said that I didn't have a brain in my head.

Farther along the road to success and distinction, I became involved in a matter having to do with the rights of property owners. A refining company decided to locate near Hattiesburg and did not ask, but demanded, that a family let them have a certain tract of land for their site. The family declined, and the company told them that they were going to take the land—and set out to try. Local tempers flared.

My contention was that I'd like to see the industry locate in the area, but more important than a few dozen additional jobs was the fact that the right of private ownership must not be denied. I fear my position was once again misunderstood. It was thought I was opposed to industry moving in; thus I was said to be against additional payrolls for the area. A few advertisers saw fit to cancel because of my position; among them the refining company and two other firms in the petroleum business, all of which were good advertising accounts. When it was all over the right of the property owners was retained and the refinery located in the area anyway. I was not invited to the formal opening.

Probably my greatest single step toward my present distinction was taken in March of 1956. Around the first of the month I learned that a citizens council group was going to be organized in Forrest County. The date for organization was set for March 21. I felt inclined to oppose the council, contending that we had sufficient bigots without organizing them. I worked on editorial copy for almost two weeks, and all of it seemed inadequate to me. With my deadline approaching, I decided to run a full-page ad in behalf of the citizens councils.

I did not attend the meeting at the courthouse, not having been invited; however, a friend went in my behalf and reported to me. The keynote address was delivered by a local attorney, and at one point in his address he saw fit to hold up before the audience the page I had so generously donated. With a dramatic gesture he denounced it, finally throwing it to the floor with the statement that he was going to cancel his subscription to my paper.

Following the service I rendered in behalf of the citizens councils, there were a few telephone calls, a canceled subscription, perhaps two or more. Those telephone calls were interesting, especially the several from unidentified ladies. One lady advised my wife (I had stopped answering the telephone) to tell me not to stick my head out of the house, else her husband would knock it off. Another lady said to me: "You nigger-loving Commie, son-of-a-bitch. Somebody ought to kill you." I found it to be such a pleasure to talk with ladies. Shortly after this, however, I had to have the phone number unlisted; otherwise I would never have got any work done.

One day en route from my home in Hattiesburg to my office in Petal I stopped for a traffic light near the post office in Hattiesburg, and a gentleman of the Old South walked from the curb over to my car and said to me: "You no-good bastard, if you'll get out of that car I'll mop up the street with you." Being a natural-born coward, I told him. "Well, now, you'll have to offer me more inducement than that." While wondering what additional inducement he might offer, I drove away.

The most recent incident to bring to mind my success as a publisher and editor had to do with a congressional election in the district where I live. The congressman wrote me a letter, enclosing his formal announcement, and in the letter he said there would be advertising sent to me later. After a week or two I noticed that every single newspaper in the district had ads from the congressman—except mine. I felt inclined to check around and learned that "a Petal merchant" had called the congressman on the telephone in Washington and advised him not to run his announcement in my paper. The congressman ran his announcement anyway, but decided not to run any advertising. Later, about five or six days before the election, I got word from his headquarters that they had decided to run one ad with me. I explained that while I appreciated it, I was not upset about having been left out; that, after all, I wasn't concerned with the principle of the thing—just the money! But what bothered me most of all was the fact that "a Petal merchant" had spent that money on a long-distance telephone call; he could have run a large ad in my paper for what it cost him. Some businessmen simply amaze me.

I'm a great shake as a businessman myself. A newspaper with no local advertising and no local circulation naturally doesn't make too much money. In fact, the *Petal Paper* keeps going only because my creditors are astonishingly patient; because a good many subscriptions are beginning to flow in from outside the state; and because I pick up a little cash by lecturing.

I guess I'm never going to be much of a social success, either—but my wife and I don't let it bother us any longer. We have three or four friends who will go to the movies with us occasionally, even though we don't like to embarrass them by asking them to our house. My daughter, who is now seven, has finished her freshman year in elementary school. To date she has suffered no stings because of her father. I'm trying to teach her enough self-reliance so that she won't get an ulcer, but maybe can give them to other people, should the need arise.

I don't have any regrets—although I am sorry that I had to change ambitions along the way. My first ambition was to be a moderate in Mississippi—a rich moderate, that is. I've had to settle for being just a man of distinction.

Sauk-Prairie Sequel
Leroy Gore

Don't spit in the well—you may have to drink from it."—Russian Proverb

Country editors mostly suffer from a hallucination: they think they own their hometown. They don't. The town owns them. One 1954 morning I sat in Pete Blankenheim's barbershop, three doors from the only traffic light in Sauk City, Wisconsin, reading the *Saturday Review.* The *Saturday Review* is not the only scholarly publication available to Pete's clients. Among other things, Pete is an "egghead." He is also a persistently vocal philosopher with a great contempt for the human race, but a great respect for human beings.

In those days, if you sat in Pete's barbershop long enough you'd likely meet practically everybody of consequence in southern Wisconsin. Among the fairly regular visitors were August Derleth, Sauk-Prairie's one-man fiction factory, Frank Lloyd Wright from nearby Spring Green, and Missouri Al.

Missouri Al is the distinguished proprietor and sole owner of the only bar in southern Wisconsin where you'd best not order anything fancy like a Martini, a Manhattan, a Pink Lady or a Grasshopper. There isn't a Maraschino cherry, an olive, or a pickled onion on the premises. The way Al figures it, booze was invented to get people pleasantly looped. He leaves the vitamins to the salad industry.

That morning, however, Pete was alone, except for the stranger who had beaten me to his door by a step and a half. The stranger took off his coat, his necktie, his collar, and he unbuttoned his shirt. It is rumored that a partial striptease is a sort of tribal ritual among the male clients at metropolitan tonsorial parlors. But in rural Wisconsin we natives manage to get our whiskers and hair harvested practically fully dressed. Neckties are mostly reserved for Sundays, weddings, and funerals. Novelist Augie Derleth used to append a footnote to the brochure advertising his

Reprinted from *Grassroots Editor* 1, no. 3 (July 1960): 12–13, 18.

availability for lectures: "An additional fee of $5 will be charged if the lecturer is required to wear a necktie."

For a moment Pete and I were torn between a suspicion that the stranger might have been stung under his shirt by a hornet, and the most terrifying alternative that we'd been invaded by a fugitive from a nudist camp. But just as our eyes were about to pop from our skulls, the stranger stopped in the nick of time and climbed into the barber chair. I opened the magazine, but my eyes really weren't on its pages.

A sign hung over Pete's barber chair:

"Haircuts with Conversation $1.25, Haircuts without Conversation $1.75." It was supposed to be a gag, but the stranger apparently had been deprived of a sense of humor, among other things. He slapped a dollar bill, a silver half-dollar, and a quarter into Pete's astonished hand.

"Now," he said with a self-satisfied smirk, "keep your dam' trap shut while you trim my hair."

This I had to see. It was possible for Pete to trim a head of hair in eighteen minutes under pressure. Compelled to remain silent for half that long, it was entirely possible that he might explode from internal combustion. I lay the magazine aside, and prepared to sprint for the door the moment he developed symptoms of atomic disintegration.

The stranger, blissfully unaware of his peril, spoke to me above the whirring of the neck clippers: "Say, isn't this the town where that editor who tried to recall McCarthy lives?"

"Seems to me," I said, "I vaguely recall some such event."

"How does he stack up with the natives?" the stranger persisted.

Pete, wielding the clipping shears, had turned a lovely deep purple, but I was enjoying myself immensely at this point. I wasn't certain which side the stranger was on, but I chanced to recall a brilliant device once employed by the late Gene Talmadge when he was backed into a corner on a similarly controversial question: "Some of my friends are for it, some are against it . . . I stand with my friends."

"You'd find plenty of support for your opinion here," I observed cautiously.

"I bet I would," the stranger grunted. "If they need any help running him out of town, I'll be glad to pitch in . . . I'm against him."

From this point onward, the conversation got progressively more embarrassing. Not because of his low opinion of me, but because of the deception by which I had provoked that opinion. So chagrined was I that I failed to observe the arrival of Missouri Al until he spoke, and when Missouri Al spoke most of the windows rattled in the entire block. "Mister," he thundered, "here in Sauk we ain't against nothin' or nobody . . . we're just for decency."

At this point Pete reached inside the sheet and dropped a half-dollar inside the stranger's shirt pocket. "It's worth a half-buck," he declared, "just to say, Amen." My glow of virtue lasted three days. It expired when another stranger greeted me at the same location. This time the stranger was on my side.

"I'm proud," he gushed, "to shake the hand of the man who foiled the pope's ambition to make his stooge, Senator McCarthy, ruler of all America. Down with the Romans!" This time, nobody had to pay Pete Blankenheim to keep his mouth shut. We looked at each other, a little sick. I was a Protestant, and Pete a "fallen-away Catholic," but we lived in a largely Catholic community where the rights of the individual had been almost fiercely defended for at least three generactions.

I had learned surprisingly little in a half century, but perhaps this lesson had been worth the tuition: demagogues are not indispensable to progress, but they are probably inevitable at the present state of our evolutionary development. The tragic weakness of the demagogue, even when he chances to be on the right side, is his inability to negotiate a peace after the war is won. Small towns are small worlds. Some of those who had honestly opposed me could not forget; some of those who had supported me could not forgive their neighbors so long as the symbol of their spent passions existed. As their editor, I was the symbol.

Shortly afterward I sold the *Sauk-Prairie Star* to young, alert Robert Anderson and his father. At this moment the gentleman who had launched the "Door for Gore" movement some months previously was the leading candidate for state commander of the American Legion. In Washington, D.C. he informed the panting press that the Andersons would be permitted to stay in business

in Sauk City so long as "they kept their nose clean." At the legion
convention he was soundly defeated. At long last, Wisconsin had
rejected its most spectacular "ism."

With the exception of Pete Blankenheim, a very wise man, I'm
not sure that Sauk City understood why the sale of the *Star* was
as necessary as the recall effort to a simple soul like me. Paraphras-
ing an ancient nugget of wisdom:

Heaven preserve me from the demagogues on my side.

I went to Iowa to follow the Russian farm delegation through
the Iowa cornfields. In the welcome shade of a spreading elm one
hot July noon, I addressed a stupid question to one of the Russians:
"Are your intentions as peaceful as you'd like us to believe they
are?"

The Russian looked a little grim as he listened to the translation.
"What makes you think," he retorted, "that we Russians like to
be blown up by atom bombs any better than Americans do?"

I hadn't meant to be rude. It just hadn't occurred to me up
to this point that the Russians might have the same regard for
human lives, including their own, that we have. I began to observe
other shocking symptoms that the Communists might belong to
the human race after all. They seemed to sweat when they were
hot, smile when they received good news from home, and scowl
when they received bad news.

That night I wrote a long letter to the Soviet embassy in Washington, strongly recommending myself as a gentleman of sterling
virtue and flawless manners. Some weeks later I was granted what
I believe to be the first visa for unrestricted travel in the Soviet
Union.

My chummy relations with the Soviets were of short duration,
but it was a great experience while it lasted. Less than three days
after I had arrived in Minsk, and had been bounced over a neglected
cow path to a collective farm, the Russians decided that absence—as
far as Helsinki, Finland, anyway—makes the heart grow fonder.

I'm not sure why. Perhaps the ill-fated Geneva Conference, then
in session, had something to do with it. Perhaps the Soviets were
taking their pique against the late Mr. Dulles out on me. I'd fortified
myself with one of those phonographic courses in Russian. These
vodka garglers weren't going to put anything over on me! The

trouble was, the Russians didn't explain in Russian or any other language. The Russian equivalent of "Scram" wasn't included in my 78-r.p.m. short course, but I had no difficulty understanding them.

Back in Copenhagen, I shed the sunshine on my somewhat frantic personality on Boris Khriatchkov. Boris was the Russian consul in charge of visas. He was a short, stocky, very blond young man with the ruddy, freshly scrubbed appearance of a second string quarterback on the St. Olaf College football team. He was a few pounds short of the accepted weight for first string backfield prospects. I hoped Boris would help me get my visa reinstated. He insisted he was trying. Almost the entire able staff of the American embassy was trying, too.

On an impulse one morning, I phoned Boris to invite him and his wife to dinner at the Hotel d'Angleterre that evening. Boris was audibly shocked. He asked me to wait for my answer. I reasoned he had to ask permission from Moscow. In the light of recent reflection, it's more likely he had to ask his wife, even as you and I.

He did ask his wife—or Moscow, if you prefer to think of it that way—and we had dinner together. We talked about the things you and I would talk about. They talked about their son in Moscow, their consuming curiosity about life in America—not about our atom bombs or our military installations, but about our automatic washing machines, our supermarkets, our forty-hour week. Even though Boris had spent some time at United Nations, I suspected that all he had seen of America was the inside of his hotel room, the inside of American elevators, the inside of Yellow Cabs and the inside of the U.N. chambers.

I tried very hard to describe Sauk City with its telephones, bathtubs, and central heating in practically all of its homes. I'm sure they privately considered me to be the greatest spinner of fairy tales since Hans Christian Andersen, but they were too polite to say so.

I heard vague rumors that after the revolution Boris had done some very bad things. Perhaps the rumors are true. In the frenzy of violence and fear, it may be possible for very good men to act very badly. I do not know. I do know that Boris had a great many fine qualities.

I made one last, futile trip to Helsinki seeking re-admission into Russia. Two days before Christmas I cabled Boris that I was going home. He and his wife were waiting at Copenhagen airport when I arrived. I had very little time between planes. They begged me to stay a little longer. "I am sure Moscow will realize that you are a good man and let you return to our beautiful country," Boris pled.

But I'd had my fill of waiting, especially at Christmas time. I bade them good-bye. They insisted on walking to the gate with me in the chill, drizzling rain. I bade them good-bye again and sprinted for my plane, not a moment too soon. The engines were already throbbing as I settled in my seat. Through the rain-streaked windows I saw Boris and his wife, still weeping and waving and soaked to the skin. I waved back at them. The SAS airliner thundered down the runway, and suddenly we were airborne. Boris, his wife, and the lights of Copenhagen disappeared in the darkness behind me.

Three weeks after Christmas the American embassy in Copenhagen contacted me at Sauk City, Wisconsin, U.S.A. Apparently Boris had got through to Moscow. The Russians would tolerate my return—but this time through Vienna, please. The Russians not only excel in outerspace exploration. They're miles ahead of us in "red tape." But naturally!

The following year, I ran for Congress. This was a blunder of colossal proportions, even for a blundering expert like me. The Third Congressional District of Wisconsin hadn't elected a Democrat since 1904, and I was a Democrat after fifty years of unflinching Republicanism.

If I'd been elected by some unlikely miracle, I doubt if I could have endured all those speeches anyway. In losing, the fees were somewhat higher than I could afford. Furthermore, I wince a little these days when I read some of my own campaign speeches. I shudder to admit it, but I'm afraid that even I have a wee bit of the demagogue in me. Fortunately, I'm a remarkable inept demagogue, but like my pappy used to say, "The only good demagogue is a bad one."

Obviously, in sixty hours I didn't become a Russian expert, anymore than I became a European expert in five months or, for

that matter, anymore than I've become an expert on America in
fifty-five years.

But I did come home from Russia and Europe with a new respect
for the much maligned American farmer; and a conviction that
our abundant food supplies—about which we have complained with
un-Christian vigor—have been a greater deterrent to war than our
atom bombs.

The Russians have atom bombs; their food supplies were inadequate for more than a few weeks of all-out warfare. They had
starches in abundance. The Ukranians are excellent wheat farmers.
What they know about wheat is exceeded only by what they don't
know about cattle, hogs, and corn. You can accept that as the
considered judgment of a tough old cowhand from Iowa and Wisconsin. I don't pretend to know much about people, but I know
a great deal about cows and hogs.

The Russians were, and I'm sure they still are, woefully short
of proteins and fats. Unlike Kaiser Wilhelm and Adolph Hitler,
the Russian leaders could not hope to confiscate large food supplies
in the low countries. These days the low countries operate in an
agricultural economy of carefully controlled near-scarcity and
carefully controlled prices. Only in America is food plentiful and
cheap.

I've taken a long, hard look at the American farmer. When I
was young, thirty Americans in every one hundred were busily
occupied in the production of food. Today, ten citizens out of every
one hundred produce more than we can eat.

Milk sells for twenty-two cents a quart in my hometown. The
farmer receives eight cents a quart. Under the same processing
and distribution system, we'd pay fourteen cents a quart for bottled
water. If any industry in America has done a better job of cutting
costs and increasing efficiency, I haven't heard of it. The farmer
is in economic hot water because he's done too good a job too
quickly, and because he's been the victim of a confused press and
confused politicians. Three thousand years ago Joseph substituted
food surpluses for weapons to build a powerful Egypt. Today, we
don't know what to do with an abundance of food in a world
where half the population goes to bed hungry every night. In the
history books of the future we'll doubtless be known as "The

Generation Which Complained Because We Had Too Much."

In 1958 I began publication of *Down on the Farm*, a photo-newspaper dedicated to the dignity of the soil and the people who till it. Unwittingly, the American farmer has made a greater contribution to American "culture" than he or the public suspects. Because food is so cheap and abundant in America, Americans have money to spend for books, magazines, newspapers, TV and radio sets, recreation, travel, and education.

In my passion for American agriculture, which predates and surpasses some of my more widely publicized activities, I presume that I may sometimes make noises like a demagogue. I try very hard not to, but unhappily our language is better adapted to labels than it is to logic. But even during those rare moments when I am temporarily convinced of my own intellectual perfection, and the thorough stupidity of those who disagree with me, I have never been tempted to spit in the well of human freedom. I drink from it too often!

This, perhaps, is the point at which the dangerous demagogue parts company with the rest of us. He doesn't hesitate to spit in the well. It never occurs to him that he may want to drink from it.

Crusades Are Not Cheaper by the Dozen

Mabel Norris Reese

Almost thirteen years ago, when I embarked upon my career as a "grass roots" editor, I had a fuzzy idea about two or three days spent at the office which would earn for me enough money to hire my housework done and allow to me time enough to enjoy my six-year old daughter and participate in community life. I was accustomed to the grind of daily journalism, issuing a weekly would be a snap—so I thought in 1947.

Reprinted from *Grassroots Editor* 1, no. 1 (January 1960): 19–21.

In those twelve-plus years since, I have found that life on a
weekly is where you bed down your children on the stacking table
while you toil into the night following a week in which there were
six eighteen-hour days, and you dread the one that follows press
day more than any others. It's payday—generously so for everyone
but the owners.

Perhaps, though, it wouldn't have been like that in those dozen
years if I had minded my business, literally speaking. Perhaps I'd
have had the time to enjoy my growing daughter, my home, and
community life if I had concentrated on the till and not worried
about the word "justice." I am certain, now, that my concern over
justice interfered with the cash register.

I was advised time and again by wiser heads than mine to watch
out for the pitfalls of "taking a stand"—that to mount a high
platform of principle was taking a downward plunge economically.
I refused to listen, and so I am badly bruised by all the plunges
I have taken.

But I could not have done it any other way. That's why now
I have two jobs. It takes two if you're going to operate as a would-be
big city journalist in the grass roots: one to eat on while the other
tends to its crusading.

I'm not real sure when I began to realize the economic pinch.
Maybe it was the first time I innocently used the editors prerogative
(to make a choice in a gubernatorial race, and I backed the wrong
man)—economically. At least, he was not the choice of the powers
that be in my town, and so I lost, for awhile, a steady advertiser.
But my man got elected, and with a good majority from my town.
It was quite awhile before that account came back.

Then came the election for sheriff of my county. A few days
before the election, the incumbent—backed by the powers that
be—hit and killed a pedestrian. I exposed the facts about the
accident as related to me by a highway patrolman, including the
one that the sheriff had been in "an eating and drinking place"
just moments before. That earned me a dressing down, and a real
cold shoulder treatment as I made my advertising rounds for the
next issue.

The sheriff was reelected and the war was on. When he shot
and killed one Negro prisoner and seriously wounded another while

returning them from the state prison for trial, I opened both barrels. I covered the inquest in which the sheriff contended the Negroes had tried to escape, and I used all the language at my command to describe the wounded Negro and relate his account of the shooting. Our printing plant began to suffer from lost revenue.

Came then 1954, and the Supreme Court's desegregation decision. My next issue carried an editorial in defense of the principle behind it, and a recommendation for gradual desegregation. And I pleaded for tolerance; for cool heads to guide the transition.

There was an explosion of fire in my yard soon after this—flames licked at a great, gasoline-soaked wooden cross that had been planted there. Two nights later, the *Topic*'s office windows were smeared with big red crosses and beneath them were the initials "KKK."

A few weeks later, I was launched on a real crusade. Five children had been enrolled in Mount Dora's public school, and from my daughter I learned that a slight uproar had been stirred about them. There were complaints, she said, that they seemed like Negroes. But the furor died when the principal investigated their background and found they had attended a white school in their ntive North Carolina, and they were, in fact, of Indian descent.

But this explanation did not satisfy the sheriff. He said they looked like Negroes. He said he didn't like the shape of the nose of the oldest girl. So he ordered them out of the school. I went on their trail and got the complete story and took pictures—sad pictures of the girl reading a book on American democracy, and of the little children clinging to the knees of their worried father.

I gave the story banner treatment, and on the editorial page I blasted the sheriff into the next county. It looked as if I had him. It looked as if he finally was impaled upon my editorial pen. I went out on my next advertising rounds fully expecting the powers that be to say—"Well, I guess you had him pegged all along."

Instead, the shoulders were much colder; the advertisers were all so very busy; the customers were all well stocked with printing. And not a one of them mentioned the *Topic*'s big exposé. I went back to my office and blazed forth another feature story about the Platt children and how happy they were over a Thanksgiving turkey a kind soul (me) had sent them, and I took many more pictures.

Meanwhile, *Time* magazine moved in, and the *Topic*'s exposé became national news. Florida dailies moved in, too, and the state soon was buzzing. The *Miami Herald* wanted to do something a bit different, so it moved in and did quite a story about the "feud" between the sheriff and the lady editor, shedding not a tear about the five children who were not allowed to go to school. The atmosphere became horribly chilly.

The word justice, though, seemed to come out of my typewriter automatically. I could not leave it alone. Finally, it became so capitalized on the *Topic*'s pages, that it met the eyes of enough people that money began to roll in for a defense fund. Lawyers took the case, and we filed suit to get the children back into school. That kept the *Platt* case live, so that scarcely an issue of the *Topic* in the months that followed came forth without a story on it.

Then the ax fell—or at least it struck a blow. I learned that the powers that be had got together and brought in a rival newspaper. The *Mount Dora Herald* sprung to life, with an office right across the street from mine, and with the printing farmed out—not to the *Topic*, of course. I had to sit in my office and watch the sheriff going in that office regularly to confer with the new publisher.

My husband and I tightened our belts and waded deeper into the fight. I made my advertising rounds as usual and picked up the crumbs. And he printed scratch pads and tablets in lieu of the printing orders we no longer had. Somehow, we made it through that dreadful summer, still aiming our sights on the word "justice."

A year from the date of our exposé, we gleefully ran what we hoped would be the last Platt story: the finale of the case in which the judge ruled that the sheriff had produced no evidence to sustain his "charge" against the children, and that they were entitled to attend any white school of their choice. But there was an anticlimax or two. An attempt was made by night riders to burn down the Platt home, and a couple of air force practice bombs were tossed into our yard.

Meanwhile the opposition paper was hard at work trying to roast me in the chilled business atmosphere. Unmercifully, it attacked me in its editorial columns, all but spelling out the hints that I was a Communist. It turned the inch given it by the powers that be into a mile of rope, and it hung itself. People became indignant, and they became increasingly more so when I refused to answer back. Rumblings were heard throughout the town, and I am sure they reached the ears of the business people.

Ads began to disappear from that paper. More and more copies of it were found in the post office wastebasket. At last, its swan-song issue appeared, and accompanying the final, dying gasp at me was an editorial that blasted those who had not "kept their promises." I bid it farewell with a 14-point head that merely said the *Mount Dora Herald* had ceased publication.

Peace did not return for me, however. A truce, yes—but a truce as uneasy as any the Middle East suffers, I still called shots on elections, and I still managed to back the "wrong" candidates. And I still fought for justice in cases involving the sheriff.

There's a new one right now—one in which I am blasting him for an act so unjust that—but let us not bore you with the details. Sufficient it is to say I am again feeling the chill, despite Florida's wonderful climate.

I know the why of it in my case, of course. Here, the sheriff is regarded as the one man who can "protect" the white people from integration. And he's considered the one man who can keep the labor unions from doing anything about the low wages in the citrus industry. So he is backed blindly by the powers that be.

But what I can't understand fully about a typical American community, such as mine, is the lack of concern for justice. I can't understand why it is felt that a community newspaper should not enter into campaigns for justice or should not even take a stand in an election.

Communities like this still form the backbone of America, and here should be the fertile testing ground for democratic principles. For here, the people are close and interdependent. Here, if help is needed, there is no government bureau at hand to dole it out without compassion, so it must come from neighbors, and it should come embellished with compassion.

The people, in a vague sort of way, realize this, I believe. At any rate our circulation did not suffer during the Platt case—for each punishment cancellation we received, sales at newsstands went up accordingly. And the normal pace of growth was accelerated by curiosity seekers from other towns.

The people, I am convinced, were interested—but they wanted only to be bystanders. They did not relate the problem of upholding justice to themselves; they could not see that where it can be denied successfully to a lowly one among them, the next time it could creep a notch higher up the economic pole. Except for a quickly squelched protest of a teen-age Sunday School class over the treatment given the Platt children, the churches were silent. However, when it was all over, an adult Sunday School class did pass a resolution naming me "Woman of the Year." I was deeply grateful, but all I could think of was how much that resolution would have helped me economically had it been issued in the height of the crusade.

What of the business community in such instances? Really, I do understand the attitude, while at the same time scorning it. Business in a town the size of Mount Dora—about five thousand then—has a constant struggle. Dailies coming into the community carry advertising from the "big city" to lure their customers; they are plagued also by competition from the next town, just five miles away. Indeed, while a newspaper may deem it a duty to mind the business of justice, the average merchant feels it a matter of life and death to mind his own business.

If he takes sides with justice, he knows he would offend the editor's enemies; if he withdraws even the crumbs of advertising, he knows he would offend the editor's friends. So he remains mute, hoping it will all go away and let him capture as much of the town's trade as he possibly can. A firm, decisive stand taken by him on the side of justice might have kept the agony from being prolonged; might have made the sheriff draw in his horns—but the average merchant is afraid of such a drastic step.

His mind works to the tune of the cash register, not to the beat of his heart. I understand this—but I could never mimic it. So that is why I also work for the *Daytona Beach News-Journal* as an editorial writer.

Does a Printer Have the Right to Print What He Chooses?

Lawrence Lorenz

> Printers are educated in the Belief, that when Men differ in Opinion, both Sides ought equally to have the Advantage of being heard by the Publick; and that when Truth and Error have fair Play, the former is always an overmatch for the latter: Hence they chearfully serve all contending Writers that pay them well, without regarding on which side they are of the Question in Dispute.
>
> That it is unreasonable to imagine Printers approve of every thing they print, and to censure them on any particular thing accordingly; . . . and End would thereby be put to Free Writing.—Benjamin Franklin. "An Apology for Printers." 1731

Does a printer have the right to print what he chooses, even if it offends a substantial portion of his community? William F. Schanen, Jr., is one printer who thinks so. And because he does, he is the target of an economic boycott that threatens to drive him out of business.

Schanen is the owner of Port Publications, Inc., of Port Washington, Wisconsin, publishers of three weekly newspapers in suburban Ozaukee County, just north of Milwaukee: the *Ozaukee Press,* with a circulation of 5,955 in the area surrounding Port Washington, the county seat; the *Mequon Squire,* with 1,890 circulation; and the *Grafton Citizen,* circulation, 2,000.

The newspapers and the job printing Port Publications takes on when his press would otherwise be idle have provided Schanen with a good living these last thirty years. Until this summer, the newspapers' gross advertising revenue came to about two hundred thousand dollars a year.

At the same time, Schanen's newspapers serve their communities and serve them well, and he is justly proud of the shiny new plaque that hangs in his office: first place in the National Newspaper

Reprinted from *Grassroots Editor* 10, no. 6 (November–December 1969): 8–11.

Association's 1969 General Excellence Award competition. But in providing an editorial voice for the county, Schanen has recognized that a publisher must be guided by his own lights, even when those chafe the community at large. Aware as he is that a weekly newspaper publisher must be a "good guy" to keep going, he has not been deterred from taking stands that have sometimes ired his neighbors.

Schanen is a liberal in a county that is not only predominantly conservative, but one that has pockets of rabid right-wing sentiment. Ozaukeeans have fond memories of the late Sen. Joseph McCarthy and keep alive his passion for ferreting out Communist influences in their midst; many claim membership in the John Birch Society or other right-wing organizations.

Only recently did the community finish battling the water fluoridation question, and though the motion to fluoridate passed, it did so only by the narrowest of margins. A vocal group is now hard at the task of driving sex education from the schools. In both cases, Schanen has taken stands opposite the conservatives.

In other instances, in the view of his antagonists, he has been critical of the most stable elements in the community: the police board, various ordinances, occasional school practices, "Port Publications seems to want to tear everything down," says the Reverend Gordon DeHaas, pastor of the Ozaukee Baptist Church in Cedarburg.

But the immediate source of Ozaukee County's disaffection is Schanen's printing of an underground newspaper, *Kaleidoscope*, published by members of what is generally referred to as the Milwaukee hippie community, and his refusal to exercise censorship over the newspaper's content or tear up his contract with the publishers.

The biweekly *Kaleidoscope* is filled with everything that is repugnant to Ozaukee County's—or, for that matter, any other middle-class community's—sense of tradition, dignity, and decency. Like many another underground newspaper, it is anti-Establishment in editorial policy, lashing out in its news columns against what it sees as abuses of authority by police and priests, mayors and magistrates, high school principals and university presidents. It is antiwar and propot. It also sprinkles its pages with four-letter words and occasionally prints drawings and photographs of nude men and women.

As early as last March, County District Attorney Walter Swietlik urged civic action to force Schanen to stop printing the newspaper and thus drive it out of the county. He charged that some of the editorial content in the newspaper was obscene, although he admitted that it probably was not legally obscene. Doubting that he could obtain an obscenity ruling in the courts, he did not attempt to prosecute Schanen. Instead, he called on Ozaukee countians to express to Schanen, as individuals, their displeasure.

It is doubtful that many of them had even read *Kaleidoscope*; the newspaper is not even distributed in the county. But they took Swietlik's word that it was a menace and began telephoning complaints to Schanen. For each of them, Schanen had the same reply: he was a printer, not a censor, and he would continue to print *Kaleidoscope* until it was found guilty of obscenity in the courts.

"I don't think a printer should deny his facility to a justifiable use, a proper use, a legal use," Schanen says. "We've had opportunities to print some of the most miserable junk you've ever seen, some of the dirty stuff you find on the average drugstore shelf, but we've refused." That Schanen was not budging became all too clear as the cold Wisconsin winter became spring, then summer. Especially aware of his position was a Grafton businessman named Benjamin Grob.

Grob is a self-made man, owner of Grob, Inc., manufacturers of machine tools. Now sixty-eight, he emigrated to the United States with his brother Theodore in the early 1920s, and by 1929 the two had built a small machine-tool factory in West Allis, a western suburb of Milwaukee. Eight years later they transferred operations to Grafton, and in 1955 Theodore branched out on his own and Benjamin continued Grob, Inc., by himself.

Benjamin Grob is also an admitted conservative. In 1951, after President Truman fired Gen. Douglas MacArthur, Grob and his brother closed their plant for one hour one day to protest. A member of Dr. Fred Schwarz's Christian Anti-Communism Crusade, he sells Schwarz's paperbacks at his offices. A picture of the late Senator McCarthy hangs in the building's entranceway.

Like Swietlik, Grob was convinced, courts or no courts, that *Kaleidoscope* was obscene, and he set out to take action. In June, after hearing another of Swietlik's complaints about the newspaper, Grob sent a letter to an estimated five hundred key businessmen, organizations, and individuals, in which he called for an economic boycott of Port Publications.

In the letter, Grob characterized Schanen as a publisher who "prints obscene literature for profit," and to back up his charge he included a reprint of a *Kaleidoscope* article which had suggested that demonstrators disrupt Roman Catholic church services by shouting obscenities and burning communion wafers; that they have sexual intercourse at a church altar; that police are inhuman (pigs) and should be harassed by reporting fake emergencies and by writing holdup notes on the back of bank deposit slips for use by unsuspecting patrons.

Like similar articles that have appeared in *Kaleidoscope* and other underground newspapers, this one was not serious in advocating such activities; it was designed solely to "put on" and outrage the Establishment enemy and provide a laugh for the anti-Establishment.

Grob took it seriously and was outraged. "The purpose of this literature is to demoralize our youth," he wrote. "Under the heading 'In Church' it tells young people to attend church to interrupt services in a shocking way, doing things so filthy they cannot be mentioned. Under the heading 'The Police,' it claims that police officers are not human beings. It advises how to sabotage the police in general.

"Concerned citizens who contacted Mr. Schanen were told that Mr. Schanen is glad to make a fast buck, and there is nothing illegal in what Mr. Schanen does. There is nothing illegal about what I will do—I will not buy space in his newspapers, and I will not buy from anyone who advertises in his newspapers. Ladies and Gentlemen, I am looking for company."

Grob was not long in finding company. More than half a dozen local firms canceled their advertising in the Port Publications newspapers. Joseph Biever, who runs a Port Washington appliance store, and his brother Vernon, manager of the Ben Franklin store, both canceled. So did Joseph Leider, a town druggist. Orville Bathke of Home Realty dropped his firm's advertising, bringing a particularly bitter reaction from Schanen.

"I supported him when he ran for the office of Port Washington mayor," Schanen says, "In doing this, I lost the friendship of Mayor Frank Meyer. Orville's memory is short. The mayor's is long." Larger advertisers joined the boycott. Sentry Foods, a large Milwaukee area grocery chain and Schanen's biggest account, dropped him. The Wisconsin Electric Power Co., a public utility, followed suit.

Almost immediately, Schanen's gross advertising returns plunged from $3,000 a week to $700; at that rate, the boycott would cost him more than $165,000 a year. Fourteen of the thirty-nine newsstands which carried his newspapers refused to handle them, cutting into his circulation. Some subscribers also quit him, although new subscriptions from sympathizers nearly made up for that loss.

Small and large advertisers alike appeared motivated by the same considerations. One, ostensibly, was economic; to continue advertising in Port Publications would hurt their sales, they said. On the other hand, the individuals responsible for placing advertising were just as offended by *Kaleidoscope* as their neighbors. As W. W. Glish, advertising manager for the electric company put it, "I don't believe in supporting this kind of material."

About eight hundred patrons of the companies pledged their support of the boycott at a meeting at the Grafton High School in early July, and at the meeting their opposition took a definite form: the hippie movement is abetted by the Communists, *Kaleidoscope* is an integral part of the hippie movement, therefore the newspaper is tied up with the Communist conspiracy, no matter how tenuously, and must be done away with. The boycott, then, in the words of J. Douglas McKay, a former Republican state assemblyman, was "basic Americanism." And to a man, the opposition appeared to share a concept of the press later expressed by Thomas Kacmarcik, president of Cedarburg's Milsteel Products Co.:

"A printer normally should not censor what he prints, *such as the wording of an advertisement* [italics mine], if it is generally acceptable to the community," Kacmarcik said in a local television debate. "But when there's a question of danger to the community involved, then the printer should censor objectionable material."

Fortunately, not all of Schanen's neighbors agreed. About thirty of them came to his aid with an organization they called the Committee for a Free Press in Wisconsin. They took out ads in Port Publications newspapers, gathered contributions for the newspapers, distributed handbills pleading for subscribers, and located Milwaukee distributors and supporters. The mayor of Mequon joined in by allowing the committee the use of city hall for a meeting, then showed up himself. A law student at the University of Wisconsin formed a similar group, Friends of William Schanen, and began to collect money to help him in his fight. The National Newspaper Association established a fund to buy full-page ads in Schanen's newspapers.

Schanen got moral support from other organizations. The Wisconsin division of the American Civil Liberties Union condemned the boycott as "contrary to the spirit and tradition of constitutional freedom." Fifteen faculty members of the University of Wisconsin School of Journalism issued a statement in which they said, "Freedom to express only popular opinions is no freedom at all." Among the signers were the school's director, Harold L. Nelson, and a former director, Professor Emeritus Ralph O. Nafziger, now executive secretary of the Association for Education in Journalism.

Editorial backing came from numerous state newspapers, including the prestigious *Milwaukee Journal.* In an editorial on July 1, it attacked the boycott as "economic vigilantism," and in the process drew a challenge from Grob: if the *Journal* would reprint the *Kaleidoscope* article he had mailed out, he would give the *Journal* one hundred thousand dollars. Replying in a news story reporting the offer, Editor Richard H. Leonard said the *Journal,* as a family newspaper, could not be persuaded to print the article for any amount of money. "We would not take the language of this *Kaleidoscope* story into *Journal* homes," he said. "On the other hand, we defend the right, under the freedom of the press provision of our Constitution, for *Kaleidoscope* to write and a printer to print anything that is considered legal by our courts," Leonard said.

In a lengthy editorial, the *Journal* elaborated on Leonard's position. It termed the boycott "a strange, repressive version of Americanism" and restated basic principles of press freedom. It added: "Many of the boycott enthusiasts express fear of forces seeking to overthrow the nation. They fail to realize that their strategy of liberty shriveling reprisal is one way a free society can overthrow itself."

Grob and his friends are not listening, however; and no amount of moral support, nor finger-in-the-dike financial aid, will make up for Schanen's lost advertising revenue. And that revenue will not return until Schanen turns *Kaleidoscope* out. Nevertheless, the printer is standing firm. Whether he can overcome Ozaukee County's ignorance and intolerance is a matter of conjecture, although at the moment it seems unlikely that he can afford to continue much longer.

Whatever Schanen's fate, there is a terrible irony about the whole affair and it lies precisely in his opposition's appeal to "basic Americanism." In their attitudes toward the press they share a kinship with colonial Americans, who, as Professor Leonard Levy has written, "simply did not understand that freedom of thought and expression means equal freedom for the other fellow, especially the one with the hated ideas."

It would be tragic if another historian two hundred years hence would be able to say the same of us. But he might. For if Schanen's business does fail, or short of that, he is forced to cancel his *Kaleidoscope* contract in order to survive, how many other misguided zealots of whatever persuasion will seize on the boycott as a weapon against printers? And how many printers will be immune?

The *Arkansas State Press:* Squeezed to Death

Armistead S. Pride

The 1940s were plush times for Negro publications. The ebullient wartime climate sent newspaper circulations soaring to their all-time high (in excess of two million weekly), and new papers appeared

Reprinted from *Grassroots Editor* 3, no. 1 (January 1962): 6–7.

at the rate of three a month in 1945 alone. In March, 1940, twenty-eight publishers came together in Chicago and organized the Negro Newspaper Publishers Association, which soon launched its own newsgathering service and began observing the 1827 birth of Negro newspapers with National Negro Newspaper Week.

The decade saw the birth, on a five-hundred-dollar loan, of John H. Johnson's *Negro Digest,* which, in turn, bankrolled his skein of astutely selected magazines. Three agencies for garnering national advertising strictly for the Negro press opened offices during the ten-year span. The aggressive assertiveness of the weeklies drew the critical attention of columnists like Westbrook Pegler and of national magazines; the crossfire of charges and countercharges extending over several years telescoped public gaze on a lively sector of the American press.

The *Arkansas State Press* was one of twelve Negro weeklies that started in 1941. It was the second to come alive in Little Rock in the young decade and the 118th Negro news organ in the state since the short-lived *Arkansas Freeman* was launched in the same city in 1869.

Unlike the pedestrian black newspaper of the South, the *State Press* eschewed timidity. It subscribed to the prevailing slogan: militancy sells papers. A shorthorn bull centered in a profile design of the state graced the middle of its nameplate. The masthead left no doubt as to its intentions. "A reader's paper, non-political, non-sectarian, independent, constructive, and with a program to integrate the Negro in all phases of community activities as American citizens." That meant rubbing the fur of many citizens the wrong way.

The *State Press*, a sixteen-page tabloid selling at fifteen cents, gave high priority to city and state coverage. Its editorial page was hard-hitting and blunt, focusing its readers' eyes week after week on the disparity in racial legal and extralegal provisions and the need for unrelenting Negro vigilance. Each week in 120-point letters the center of the front page headlined the number-one story: "Attempt to Destroy the Bateses, Fails," or "Court Halts State Aid to Perpetuate JIMCRO Schools; to Act Further in May." From two to four other heads filled out the page.

Light on society and blind to sports, the *State Press* blanketed schools, churches, and organizations. It brightened its pages with a sprinkling of comic strips and fashion hints. Its several Negro-angled cartoon panels had point: "Look nice but do your dressing at home," not on the streetcar; a warning to keep dogs off the streets when children are on vacation from school; global advice to Uncle Sam to clean up the "filth [division of races, Negro-white tensions, etc.] in your yard." For filler it chose such expressions as: "Trade where you can work"; "Stand by the Press—It stands by you"; "Don't support jimcro"; "Don't get mad, Get smart—Join the NAACP." In one issue it drew upon Heywood Broun: "Perhaps the first thing needed for a liberal paper is capital, but even more important, is courage."

The *State Press* unhesitatingly belabored the Negro for his lethargy. One editorial, "What Is the Negro in Arkansas Waiting on?" came up with a twofold answer to the question. The large Negro state teachers organization, replete with elaborate headquarters, staffed with legal counsel and paid executive director, had not, it said, done anything about anti-Negro legislation because it was waiting on the NAACP to carry the ball. When officials after election turned their backs on Negro interests, Negro political groups, the editorial went on, stood limp because "God would take care of it." The NAACP cannot attend to all of the Negro's ills, said the *State Press*, and "It is our sincere belief that God will crown you with knowledge and ability, and if you don't use it to help yourself, brother,you are going to continue to find yourself in one 'mell of a hess.' "

The publishing team of L. Christopher Bates, and his wife, Daisy, who was later to become head of the state conference of NAACP branches and to make national headlines as she led Negro children to storm-tossed Central High School, eyed a clientele of 22,103 local and 408,303 state (majority rural) Negroes. The first-day press run (May 9) was fifteen hundred; three months later it was twice that. Arkansas circulation alone climbed to twenty thousand by 1957, then dwindled to five thousand in 1959. Trouble was at hand and the paper ceased publication, the victim of a direct advertising squeeze.

It was not the first time advertisers put pressures on the *State Press*. In 1942 its unrelenting crusade in behalf of individual rights and constitutional law drew the ire of downtown merchants, and its exposé of a policeman who had maliciously killed a Negro soldier on West Ninth Street, the Negro business strip, irked them no end. They put the paper out of bounds for their advertising. The *State Press* forthwith transferred its solicitors from advertising to circulation sales. The paper steadily acquired more readers, both white and Negro, and became an irresistible medium for the market-wise merchant.

Representatives of a Little Rock organization of businessmen offered to bargain with the *State Press* publishers. The merchants would return to the ad columns if the paper softened its tone. The *Press* replied that where Negro interests were involved, there would be no compromise.

Eventually the advertisers came back. This was a voluntary move inasmuch as from 1942 until its death, the *Press* did not solicit an ad from a white merchant. The newspaper enjoyed a healthy life in both advertising and circulation until 1957, its peak year, when controversy developed over a court decision ordering Little Rock schools to integrate. Earlier, in 1954, when the U.S. Supreme Court rendered its historic school desegregation decision, efforts to stifle the *Press* served only to bring the paper more ads and increased sales. But the 1957 affair was a different matter. It hit home and the local segregationists went hunting. What better target than the archchampion of integration, of desegrated schools, the sixteen-year-old *State Press*?

The Bateses endured two years of ulcer-breeding harassment—telephone threats, blood-signed letters, pistol shots, Ku Klux cross-burnings on the lawn, nightriding rock-throwers. "The number of times that the marauders have struck is too numerous to record," stated the *Press*. "Property damage would run into the thousands." Late in April of 1958 a missile dashed through the front window of the Bates home on West Twenty-eighth street bearing the message, "Rock this time, dynamite next time."

The Bateses erected iron screens on their windows and, in the absence of police protection, hired private guards. Then, at 10:08 on the evening of July 7, a bomb exploded on the Bateses' lawn, causing extensive window damage and leaving a deep crater in its wake. Midway in the combat between the *State Press* and its adversaries, the Lincoln University Department of Journalism saluted the Bateses with a citation of merit for braving "physical danger and economic loss in an unremitting fight for the underprivileged."

Failing in their efforts to scare the *Press* owners into submission by terror-breeding tactics, the anti-Bates forces resorted to the economic squeeze. With Governor Orval Faubus spearheading the antidesegregation drive, the Bateses' tormentors found themselves muscularized from a prestigious source and made the most of it. Mr. Bates wrote: "Arkansas's governor entered the picture in 1957 and used his executive powers to destroy the *Press* and his police force used gestapo methods to prevent news agents from handling the paper, and when the paper was barred from the school rooms as well as most of the communities, the circulation among both white and colored dwindled considerably."

By 1959 the circulation had plummeted to less than five thousand, and all state and city advertisers had canceled their contracts. Pressure on national advertisers from wholesale distributors in the state caused cancellation of 90 percent of the *Press*'s national advertisements. In addition to this, the *Press* had housing trouble.

The building in which the *State Press* was housed had a black owner. Local whites put pressure on the owner of the building, who in turn canceled the lease and asked the *Press* to vacate. At that time, even if funds had been available it would have been impossible to find another place that would have been sold or rented to the *State Press*.

Mr. Bates's valedictory had the dual edge of his editorial shafts: "However, in the face of editorial losses (that ran into the thousands of dollars) the *Press* was faced with one thing— the Negroes in Arkansas who would have kept the *Press* operating, could not; and those who could, would not. the former were intimidated and threatened by the white men, the latter were brainwashed by the white men."

So, with the October 29, 1959, issue without warning, the *State Press* closed its doors—survivor of terror but victim of boycott.

A Company of Bold Riders

Edgar E. Eaton

A handful of newspapermen in the country have mounted their steeds and gone off to battle against near impossible odds. Instead of sitting high in the saddle, however, they lean back in editorial chairs. Their lances are tabloid newspapers and instead of windmills they challenge real problems such as pollution, urban high-rise planning, and the population explosion. Although these idealistic editors and publishers may feel like Don Quixote or Walter Mitty at times, their battles are real and their victories, though too infrequent to satisfy most of them, are significant.

The editor of the modern "advocacy journal" is not tied down by some of the restrictions of the Establishment press, nor is he given to calling all policemen pigs and proclaiming revolution as do many in the underground newspapers. These special newspapers offer a commentary on society; every story is treated interpretatively. Some definitely slant their news rather than just interpret, but the reader knows when he subscribes to the paper he's not going to get traditional objective coverage.

In Wyoming the subscriber to the *High County News* expects to read features on hunting, fishing, and river floating and can count on editorials about preserving the environment and the bald eagle. On the West Coast the *San Francisco Bay Guardian* reader knows editor Bruce Brugmann isn't going to treat high-rise planning as straight news, and in Seattle, Philip Bailey, editor of the *Argus,* may not criticize high-rise planning but he'll tell you if he doesn't like the looks of the building you've decided to erect downtown. Up in Maine, John Cole can be depended on to "tell it like it is" about nuclear power plants or pulp and paper mills.

Most of the advocacy journals are rather new, founded within the last few years. Exceptions are the *Intermountain Observer* in Boise, Idaho, long established as the outspoken evaluator of nearly everything needing evaluating in the intermountain West; the *Argus* in Seattle, a primarily political newspaper that is old enough to have a twenty-five-years-ago column (unique among advocacy

Reprinted from *Grassroots Editor* 13, no. 3 (May–June 1972): 8–10.

journals); the late Gene Cervi's notable *Cervi's Rocky Mountain Journal* in Denver, being carried on very capably by his daughter, Clé; and the *Texas Observer* in Austin, currently publishing volume number sixty-four.

As a rule, the advocacy journals are extremely attractive tabloids. Frosty Troy's *Oklahoma Observer* and John Cole's *Maine Times* are excellent examples. Troy's paper has a four-column, 15-pica column layout, but Troy effectively uses a two-column page design on some of the inside pages. He does some unusual cropping of his art to make it fit his unique design, especially on page one.

Many of the newspapers, such as the *Maine Times*, don't justify type, setting copy flush only on the left side. When handled properly, effective use of white space is the result. The Maine newspaper is also a leader in layout of standing columns, such as art calendars, book reviews, and editorial page design.

Practically all of the advocacy journals have excellent sections devoted to coming events, the arts, and reviews of films, books, art, and poetry. Most of the newspapers are published weekly with a few coming out monthly. Summer schedules change, with several of the papers publishing less frequently during the summer months. Few are as successful as *Cervi's* which comes out twice a week.

The standard rate for a single issue is usually 25 cents a copy, although *Tompkins Chemung Bulletin* in New York is available for 10 cents. Most of the newspapers don't depend on the sale of individual copies, however, and push subscriptions which range from $2.85 for twelve issues of the monthly *San Francisco Bay Guardian* and $5.00 a year for the weekly *Tompkins Chemung Bulletin* to $20.00 annually for *Cervi's*. Most of the papers cost around $7.50 a year.

Pollution, politics, drugs, taxes, housing, education, busing, and prison reform are fairly common themes, though certainly not treated the same way in each of the various journals. The main difference between the advocacy press and the underground newspapers, other than makeup, is that the approach to the problems of the day by the advocates is more realistic and not so narrow in subject matter. An exception to the case is the *Manchester american*. (Perhaps making american lower case is a hint.) Although the New Hampshire newspaper doesn't have the gaudy, psychedelic makeup of some of the underground press, it is just as narrow in its scope. It is anti-Vietnam, proabortion (a whole issue being devoted to birth control and abortion), and for legalizing marijuana. Drugs get major attention: such as "Drug line in a community"; "Busted on the last sale," a double-truck chart on drugs and their various effects; "Turned away at the emergency room," an interpretative piece about a girl under the effects of drugs who needed help but couldn't get it at the local hospital. Other "news" is covered such as model cities, insurance rate hikes, nuclear power, and tourism in New Hampshire, but drugs and abortion get major attention.

Many advocacy newspapers editorialize and research some of the same topics emphasized by the *Manchester american*, but are more convincing because they treat the subjects as ills of society that need correcting, instead of crimes that society should be punished for.

Everything in the advocacy press is not a deadly serious crusade. Professional football—certainly not a common theme among newspapermen bent on reforming the decaying world—received attention from John Cole in the *Maine Times*. In a column from the ed page which he simply calls "John's Column" he frankly admitted enjoying the "pageantry and precision" of pro football, even though he is "nagged by twinges of guilt. I ought to be out chopping wood, walking, playing with the kids, cleaning the barn, doing something to get my gut in shape, or protecting the homestead from termites." But even though the whole multimillion dollar football business is commercial, "full of corporate pressure and politics" and "adored by middle America," Cole confessed the enjoyment he gets in front of the boob tube every weekend. "But even though Richard Nixon's sophomoric support of the Redskins has given me more cause to doubt pro football than any other single event, I still persist in enjoying the game . . . The tube is part of my time on earth."

In another issue Cole urged eighteen-year-olds to consider running for the school board to bring a necessary dimension to school administration. In another issue he paid a delightful tribute to one of those "nice old ladies" every newspaper editor knows.

Whether the advocacy journal is talking about how to grow

mushrooms or the potential dangers of nuclear power plants, it is a welcome addition to the fourth estate. And the only action that will keep them from spreading, from attracting some of the best idealists in the profession into the fold, is for the Establishment press to follow the lead and include more interpretation in areas that demand more than objectivity in covering the news. The advocacy press, in spite of a financial struggle to exist in most communities, is here to stay.

Index

Action Committee for Fair Taxes,
102
American Civil Liberties Union,
143
American Farm Bureau
Federation, 101
American Legion, 99, 127–28
American Newspaper Publishers
Association, 86
Appalachian Regional
Commission, 78–81
Arkansas Freeman, 145

Baggerly, Herbert Milton, 3
Bailey, Philip, 149
Barba, Cipriano (Philippine army
officer and newspaper
publisher), 109–14
Bartonville (Ill.) *News*, 72–76
Bates, Daisy, 146–48
Bates, L. Christopher, 146–48
Bay Area League Industrial
Association, 70
Bribery, 43
Broun, Heywood, 146
Brugmann, Bruce B., 84, 95–149
Buffalo Express, 53

California Rural Legal Assistance
Council, 92

Calomarde, Pedro
(Philippine resistance editor),
109–14
Caudill, Henry (author, *Night
Comes to the Cumberlands*), 77,
79
Censorship: of press in Vietnam,
105
Cervi, Clé, 84
Cervi, Eugene Sisto, 6, 44–45, 83,
85–105, 150
Cervi's Rocky Mountain Journal,
44–45, 84, 105, 150
Charleston (S.C.) *News & Courier*,
117
Civil liberties: abuse of, 33; fair
trial, 35, 36
Clement, Frank (governor of
Tenn.), 115
Clinton (Tenn.) *Courier News*,
117, 118
Closed meetings, 16–17, 55, 58,
69–71, 73, 75–78
Closed records: Roe Gardner's
suit for access, 61; mentioned,
69, 70–73, 93
Cloverdale (Calif.) *Reveille*, 43
Coe, Malcolm D., xv
Cole, John, 149, 151
Committee for a Free Press in
Wisconsin, 143

153

Constitutional rights: First
    Amendment, 8, 11–14, 18,
    58–61, 134, 146–47; fair trial,
    35–36; property, 122
Courier-Journal (Louisville, Ky.),
    66
Dallas Times Herald, 18. *See also*
    Jones, W. Penn, Jr.
Daytona Beach News-Journal, 137
DeCell, Hal. C., 14
Denver Post, 48, 50
Derloth, August, 125
Dover, Raye, 16, 17
Down on the Farm, 132

Eastern Kentucky Housing
    Development Corporation, 77
Editorial success: rules for, 27–28
Enos, Edith Boys, 5
Ernst, Morris, xvii

Failing Newspaper Act, 45, 85–95
Farmer and Miner (Frederick,
    Colo.), 3, 46–47, 51–53
Farmers Union, 102
Faubus, Orville (governor of
    Ark.), 29
Federal Communications
    Commission, 87
Field, Eugene, 83, 85
Food marketing: study of, 92
Fort Collins Coloradoan, 51
Franklin, Benjamin, 138
Freeman, J. R., 3, 44, 46–53. *See
    also* Oil shale investigation
Fulton County (Ky.) *News,* 66

Gardner, Ro, 60–68. *See also*
    Closed records
Garrison, James, 21
Gish, Pat, 77–81
Gish, Tom, 77–81

Golden Quill Award for Editorial
    Writing, xvi, 45, 54.
    See also DeCell, Hal; Hicks,
    Dan, Jr.; Remmenga, Alvin J.;
    Smith, Hazel Brannon
Government subsidies, 105
Grafton (Wis.) *Citizen,* 138
Grange, 102
Grassroots Editor, xiii–xx
Greeley (Colo.) *Tribune,* 51
Gutowski, Stanley, M.D., 31, 34

Hawkins, Marlin (sheriff, Conway
    County, Ark.), 29–31, 35–36,
    40–44
Health Education and Welfare,
    Department of, 64, 66
Hickman (Ky.) *Courier,* 60–66
Hicks, Dan, Jr., 53–60
High County News, 149
Hough, Henry Beetle, 3

Illinois Farmer, 108
Illinois Power & Light Company,
    106–7
Illinois Press Association, 71, 74
Integration, 114–20, 134, 136, 145,
    147–48. *See also* Minority
    groups; Race relations
Intermountain Observer (Boise,
    Idaho), 149
International Conference of
    Weekly Newspaper Editors, xvi,
    xx, 44, 54, 99
Intimidation of editors:
    vandalism, 4, 32, 43, 107, 147;
    political action, 7–8, 12–17,
    28–36; economic boycott, 8, 43,
    60, 71–72, 78–79, 107, 133–47;
    arson, 15–17, 33, 45, 52, 94,
    135; threats, 27, 64, 71, 74–79;
    115–23, 147–48; lawsuits, 31–58

passim; mob action, 32; perjury
conviction, 35-38; assassination
attempts, 51-53, 56; robbery,
56; physical assault, 56, 71-75,
100; slander, 71; bomb
explosion, 74, 116, 117, 135,
147-48; riots, 116. *See also*
American Legion; John Birch
Society; Ku Klux Klan; White
Citizens Council
–libel: judgments against, 7,
38; suits threatened, 31-32;
suits against, 43, 71-78

John Birch Society, 19, 99, 107,
139
Jones, Eugene, 80
Jones, W. Penn, Jr. (author of
Forgive My Grief), 18-25,
47-52. *See also Dallas Times
Herald*

Kadaugan, 109
Kaleidoscope, 139-44
Kasper, John Frederick, 116
Kennedy, John F., 19-23, 59. *See
also* Jones, W. Penn, Jr.
Kennedy, Robert F., 56-57, 59, 80
Kentucky Civil Liberties Union,
64-67
Kentucky Human Rights
Commission, 64-67
Kentucky River Development
Association, 78
Kilgallen, Dorothy: death of, 21
King, Dr. Martin Luther, Jr., 57
KPIX (San Francisco), 89
KRON (San Francisco), 87-91
Ku Klux Klan, 12-14, 55-56, 58,
104, 134, 147

Leonard, Richard H., 143

Levy, Leonard, 144
Lexington (Miss.) *Advertiser*, 8-14,
45
Lincoln University Department of
Journalism, 148
Littleton (Colo.) *Independent*, 5,
51-53
Lovejoy, Elijah Parish: Award for
Courage in Journalism, xvi, 33,
43, 45, 54-55; mentioned, 118.
See also Freeman, J. R.;
Gardner, Ro; Gish, Tom;
Hicks, Dan, Jr.; Jones, W.
Penn, Jr.; Newborn, A. J., Jr.;
Reese, Mabel Norris; Schanen,
William F., Jr.; Smith, Hazel
Brannon; Stagg, Bessie; Wells,
John F.; Wells, Horace V., Jr.;
Wirges, Gene
Loveland (Colo.) *Reporter*, 51

McCarthy, Sen. Joseph R.,
126-27, 137-40
Macy, Blair, 6
Maine Times, 150-51
Manchester (N.H.) *american*,
150-51
Manhattan East, 47
Medicare: administration of, 55
MeQuon (Wis.) *Squire*, 138
Miami Herald, 135
Midlothian (Tex.) *Mirror*, 4, 15,
19-21, 47
Milwaukee Journal, 143
Minority groups: abuse of, 60-68,
133-34
Mishawaka (Ind.) *Enterprise*, 3
Monroe County Democrat
(Madisonville, Tenn.), 53-60
Morgan, Howe, xvi-xvii
Morning Times (Cebu City,
Philippines), 110-14

Morrilton (Ark.) *Democrat*, 4, 29–41, 44
Morrilton (Ark.) *Headlight*, 32
Morris, DeLyte, xv–xvii
Mt. Dora (Fla.) *Herald*, 135–36
Mt. Dora (Fla.) *Topic*, 135

Nader, Ralph, 88–89
Nafziger, Ralph O., 143
National Association for the Advancement of Colored People, 146
National Farmers Organization, 101–2, 108
National Newspaper Association: general exellence award of, 138; mentioned, 45, 153
Negro Digest, 145
Negro Newspaper Publishers Association, 145
Nelson, Harold, 143
Newborn, J. A., Jr., 43
Newspaper monopoly, 84–94. *See also* Failing Newspaper Act; Newspaper Preservation Act
Newspaper Preservation Act, 85–88
Nixon, Richard M., 149

Oil shale investigation: U.S. Department of Interior, 46–49; Sen. Paul H. Douglas, 47; Senate Bills No. 1009, No. 2708, 47; Senate Committee on Interior and Insular Affairs, 47; Sen. Gordon Allott, 47–50; Rep. Wayne Aspinal, 48; Colorado legislature, 48; dawsonite claims, 48; Sen. Peter Hoyt Dominick, 50; mentioned, 51-53. *See also* Freeman, J. R.

Oil shale lands and leases, 44–47, 53
Oklahoma Observer, 150
Oswald, Lee Harvey, 20–24
Ozaukee (Wis.) *Press*, 138

Pacific Gas & Electric Company, 86–93
Paducah (Ky.) *Sun-Democrat*, 65
Parent-Teacher Association, 175
Pegler, Westbrook, 145
Peoria Journal Star, 73
Petal Paper (Petal, Miss.), 119–24
Prairie Post (Maroa, Ill.), 97-108
Public lands: alleged theft of, 3. *See also* Oil shale investigation
Pulitzer Prize, 14–15, 45

Race relations, 7–14
Radio and television licenses: investigation of, 91–92
Ramparts, 23
Reese, Mabel Norris, 118, 132–37
Remmenga, Alvin J., 43
Rockefeller, Winthrop, 34
Rocky Mountain News (Denver, Colo.), 50
Rolling Fork (Miss.) *Deer Creek Pilot*, 14
Ruby, Jack: trial of, 20–22

St. Louis Post Dispatch, 48
San Francisco Bay Guardian, 84–94, 149
San Francisco Chronicle, 87–89
San Francisco Examiner-Chronicle, 85–96
San Francisco News Call-Bulletin, 95
San Francisco Press Club, 86–87
Saturday Review, 125
Sauk-Prairie (Wis.) *Star*, 127–28

Schanen, William F., Jr., 138–44
Seattle Argus, 149
Smith, Hazel Brannon, 7–15, 45
Smith, Walter, 7–8
Society of Friends, 98–99
Southern Illinois University
  School of Journalism, 84–85
Stagg, Bessie, 69–76
Stagg, Tom, 75
Stagg, William, 73
Steffens, Lincoln, 36
Strip mining, 77–78
Suburban Journal (Clear Lake,
  Tex.), 43

Tax assessments: unfair, 102–6
Tennessee Reporter (Clinton,
  Tenn.), 117
Time, 135
Tompkins Chemung Bulletin, 150
Torch, 109
Troy, Frosty, 150
Tulia (Tex.) Herald, 3
Turnbow, Hartman, 10–12
Twain, Mark: on Tennessee
  editors, 53; mentioned, 54, 56

Valentine (Neb.) Herald, 16

Vineyard Gazette (Edgartown,
  Mass.), 3

Waring, Houstoun, xv–vi
Warren Commission Report,
  20–24
Washington Monthly, 79–80
Weekly newspaper editor:
  definition of, xiii–xv
Wells, Horace V., Jr., 54, 114–19
Wells, John F., 118
Westphaling, Mr. and Mrs. Paul,
  67
White, William Allen, 6
White Citizens Council, 7, 9, 14,
  115–23. See also Intimidation of
  editors
Whitesburg (Ky.) Mountain Eagle,
  77–81
Wilson, Eva, 97–108
Wilson, Robert E.: peace mission,
  100; on soybean price-fixing,
  101; mentioned, 98–108
Windsor (Colo.) Beacon, 49–51
Wirges, Betty, 30, 37–41
Wirges, Gene, 27–45. See also
  Intimidating of editors
Wright, Frank Lloyd, 125